FROM MOUNTAINS
TO
MOLEHILLS

OVERCOMING AND CELEBRATING YOUR DIFFERENCES IN MARRIAGE

DR. RANDY CARNEY

Overcoming and Celebrating Your Differences in Marriage

All verses cited are from the
King James Version.
This book was printed in the United States of America.
To order additional copies of this book contact:

Randy Carney, Collegiate Consulting
21086 Number 9 Blacktop
Thompsonville, IL 62890
www.RandyCarneySpeaker.com
E-Mail Address: rcarney6@gmail.com

PUBLISHED BY
FOR WORTHY BOOKS
COLUMBUS, OHIO

FWB

TABLE OF CONTENTS

WHY I WROTE THIS BOOK

I wrote this book because it deals with one of the major adjustments that any married couple will have to face.

It has often been said that opposites attract. In a lot of ways that is true. I will go into that in more detail within the chapters of this book. Part of the reason for this attraction is because we see the strengths the other person has. We admire those strengths because we see some of them lacking in ourselves. However, with each strength, there is a corresponding potential for weakness. As we get to know our spouses better, those weaknesses then become apparent. That causes some adjustment because we had not focused on those areas before marriage.

Within the pages of this book, I hope to help us understand why our spouses have different ways of thinking and different inclinations than we do. When we begin to understand how our spouses are wired in the area of personality, and how some simple things such as birth order and other factors affect our thought patterns, we are at least on our way to understanding that some of what goes on is not directed at us personally.

So, when we encounter our differences, we often have a tendency to advocate for our positions. When our spouses have different positions that area of disagreement sets us up for some potentially strong fights.

That is where we enter the area of "combat"!

That is also where the differences between us, in our perception, are like "Mountains" we have to climb.

When we celebrate on the fourth of July each year, we see glorious fireworks celebrations. While those are beautiful, we need to remember that those colorful displays were born in a full-blown war, and that many lives were lost.

When we fail to deal properly with our differences, conflict develops. Then we begin to engage in combat. In some couples that can be described as escalating into a metaphorical "full-blown war"!

On the other hand, as we continue to study that complex creature we married, we can begin to see the wonderful traits he or she possesses.

In many areas, we just need to understand that we are just different. One is not better (at least in many cases of differences this is true), just different.

When we allow each other to be who we truly are, and when we learn where to limit our liberty and show deference to each other, we can come to the point of having a tolerable marriage. Then, as we perfect this process, we can laugh at out differences. We can "cut each other some slack." We can pursue our own interests while allowing our spouses to do the same. We don't want to lead completely separate lives, so we want to support our mates in their unique interests. We want to learn about those, and spend some time sharing in those areas. Now, we are getting into the "how-to." You will see more of that in the pages of this book.

So, when faced with our differences, we can become combative, or we can step back and find different ways to deal with those differences and the frustrations they may cause. We can support our partners in their unique interests and personality traits; realizing one is not necessarily better, but just different. When we do that, instead of engaging in combat, we can come to the point of tolerating and moving on to celebrating our differences. We will move from engaging in combat to watching glorious fireworks. When that happens we will have turned our "Mountains" into "Molehills"!

WHY YOU SHOULD READ THIS BOOK

This book will help you carry out the most important commitment you can make in your marriage. In many wedding ceremonies, the couple promises to love each other and continue in the marriage in things like "in sickness and in health, for better or for worse, for richer or for poorer." My friend, Mike Meece, pointed out that what the potential groom hears when those words are said and repeated are "health, better, and richer." I suspect that it would be the same for many potential brides. The most important commitment you can make in your marriage is to overcome whatever comes your way. Part of what you will need to overcome is learning how to handle your differences.

Marriages will have many surprises and pitfalls along the way.

One of those surprises will come about when we discover, "He thinks that???" or "She feels that???" Many spouses will exclaim, "I had no idea!!!"

Oh yes, you will discover a lot of things about your husband or wife that you did not expect.

If you are contemplating marriage, you should read this book to keep you from being blind-sided.

Many of us have already gone through the experience of discovering the differences we have with our mates. Maybe, though, we have chosen the role of combat.

If you would like to change that, continue to read. Move from viewing your differences as a reason to engage in combat to viewing those differences as glorious fireworks celebrations

CHAPTER 1.

THE SIX HABITS OF HIGHLY EFFECTIVE MARRIAGES

What makes marriages successful? After many years of counseling married couples as a bi-vocational minister, I came to realize that they had developed habits of becoming successful in six different areas of marriage.

When implementing these principles in such a way that following them becomes a habit, a marriage is on its way to experiencing marital bliss.

INTRODUCTION TO THE SIX KEYS TO MARITAL BLISS

Loving to camp, I said, "Let's go camping!"

My children who ranged from about two to eight years of age at that time said, "Yea!!!!" My wife, Rhonda, did not have quite as an excited look on her face, but after a short pause, she said, "Oh, O.K."

See? I grew up in a family that went camping. We started out with tents, and eventually graduated to camping trailers. Rhonda's family, on the other hand, never went camping.

Anyone who knows Rhonda will tell you that she is one of the most positive people on earth. In fact, at one of the churches we served, she was nicknamed, "Little Miss Mary Sunshine."

Why was she not too excited and positive in this moment? It probably was because she had been on some of my camping trips before. We had been two or three times since we got married. One time we got sunburned. The ground was so hard we could not drive our tent stakes. Oh, yes, we slept on that hard ground. Sleeping on the ground was her least favorite part of camping. Therefore, she had reason not to be as excited as the children were.

So, we started on this adventure to which Rhonda had reluctantly agreed. We drove through the hills of north Georgia. Then we had truck trouble, but we coasted into a filling station that had a mechanic on duty. We got the truck fixed in about an hour, but then we were behind schedule. As we drove out of that town, we saw signs for two campgrounds. One was a national chain, but the other advertised the price as being one dollar cheaper. We headed in the direction of the less expensive one.

Three times, we had just about given up on finding this campground, but we finally got there.

I had decided that I was going to convert my wife to a love of camping. We have four children, and the youngest was very small at that time. I wanted all of us to enjoy camping.

Don't get me wrong. We started off the evening with a beautiful scene. There was a hillside below us covered with lush green grass. Then the hill or small mountain continued on above the area where we camped. We successfully pitched our tent in a location where we could hear the sounds of a bubbling brook in the background. I had selected a camping site with electricity, and I plugged in a fan. I set my wife down in a yard chair with the fan blowing on her. I cooked a gourmet meal of hot dogs. I even put a mattress in the tent, so we would not have to sleep directly on the ground.

That night, it began to rain, and then I heard a noise inside the tent. It was a raindrop falling right between my wife and me. I decided I would try an old trick. I reached up and touched the drop of water bulging through a hole in the tent roof. Then I ran my finger down the roof over toward the wall. I had heard that this would form a path, and that the rainwater would run down that path. It worked for about two minutes. Then about an inch away from the wall, the stream of water divided: Part of it ran on over to the wall and traveled down the side of the tent, which was the original plan; but about an inch away from the wall, water started to drop from the path. Then a further inch or two away from that, another stream of drops started flowing. Pretty soon, we had a line, where there were several drops of water falling down on us. We later discovered many other leaks.

When we started the evening, we enjoyed hearing the sound of a little bubbling brook not too far away behind our tent. During the night, the nice little stream sounded like it had become a roaring, raging river. It sounded like it was just getting ready to break through its banks and come and swoop us down the hill.

About three o'clock in the morning, I heard the front door of our pickup truck slam. Now I don't know if that slam really had any significance because it really was hard to shut that door. Rhonda had decided to spend the rest of the night in the truck. Needless to say, I did not convert her to a love of camping, and the next night we stayed in a motel.

We look back, and we often laugh about what happened during that camping trip. One thing we do remember, though, is that we made it through the experience. You may not have gone camping, but if you have survived some type of trial with your husband or wife, you should be encouraged to think that you can face other trials.

I would like to let the joys and pitfalls of camping remind us of important principles that can benefit any marriage. Each part of this series of books will introduce you to a certain set of principles. Each set of principles represents a key to marital bliss. If you implement all six of those types of principles successfully, not only will you have a successful marriage, but you will experience marital bliss as well!

You will notice this book is written from my decidedly Christian point of view, but anyone can benefit from the principles for marital bliss that are presented here. Some of the chapters are directed to families who are active in their local churches. If you are part of our larger audience, please keep reading, you will find the universal non-optional principles that will benefit any marriage.

Source: Microsoft Clip Art

CHAPTER 2.

DISCOVER YOUR DIFFERENCES: YOU WILL PROBABLY FIND SOME SURPRISES

Why should you read this chapter? This chapter will give you a foundation for what follows in this book. It will also give you some encouragement.

Really, you have to know the state of things before you can begin to fix something

As we go through this chapter, we will see that we are not alone in experiencing differences, and we will receive some encouragement in knowing that many people just like us have worked through our problems.

You may have entered marriage with some fairly high expectations of what it would be like. You may have had many long conversations with your husband or wife when you were dating.

Then, Boom, it hits you where you least expected it.

Really we are such complicated creatures, it would be very difficult for a couple to come together and not find some surprises.

Elizabeth stood in the bathroom, appalled. There was the tooth paste tube, squeezed right in the middle! She always squeezed hers from the very end. She was convinced this was much less wasteful because it seemed to her like she was getting all the goodies out of it.

She was so surprised. She and Ralph had many long conversations before they got married. They shared their dreams. They even got into some very deep subjects.

But this? How could she have missed something like this?

It seemed like a mountain to her, but then she realized it was really a molehill.

After all, he was actually the neat one. What surprised her, was, that with the exception of this one thing, he was sort of like the "neat freak," and she was surprised that compared to him, she felt somewhat like a slob.

In preparing for this book, I asked people to take a survey.

Now, mind you, it was not a scientific survey, and some would say the sample was relatively small. Yet, I found the answers very interesting.

This information gives real-world up-to-date content.

In the survey, 20% reported being in a second (or later) marriage. 80% of the respondents were in their first marriage. The majority of people who responded had been married longer than 16 years, and the largest group had been married for more than 30 years.

The significance of this is that we are getting input from many who have stuck it out through thick and thin. We also did get some input from those who had been married before. Widows or widowers who marry again (as well as others who were married before) have additional adjustments on which they can report.

In our survey, 26% said they had a difference in preference as to how the roll of toilet paper, or roll of paper towels, was put on. One of them liked it to have the roll to hang down in the front. The other one liked for it to hang down from the back.

Fortunately, in our case, I did not have a preference, as long as it was there. Rhonda prefers it to hang down the front.

A few years ago, I was pastoring a church, and we had a dinner after church one Sunday. Rhonda put the roll of paper towels up hanging down from the front. I noticed one of our Sunday School teachers looking at it. A few minutes later, he got up and went to the sink. When he left, the roll was hanging down from the back. Later, I noticed it had been switched back to where it was hanging down from the front. Yes, Rhonda had been back to the sink.

If this is something you both have strong preferences about, you are going to have to find a way to work out the situation. Some couples just live with however the roll was put on, and whoever replaces it just does so according to his or her preference. Some couples strike a deal. "OK, I will do this the way you like it IF you will do this (other thing) the way I like."

Again, according to the survey, 26% said that one of them likes the toothpaste tube squeezed in the middle, and the other prefers for it to be squeezed from the bottom. In our case, I like it squeezed from the bottom, but she often squeezes it in the middle.

When we were first married, the toothpaste tubes were different. Wherever you squeezed it is how it stayed when you finished. I told her about my preference, and she would often do it that way, but not always. Then a friend gave us a "Marriage Saver." That's what the product was called. It was plastic, kind of like a clothes pin. You put the bottom of the tube in it and rolled it up as it was being used. At least every time I used it, the tube would end up in my preferential position. Nowadays, most of the toothpaste tubes we use are plastic, and they just spring back into position, no matter where you squeeze them. Thank you, toothpaste manufacturers. You may have saved many marriages.

Years ago, I heard my friend, Ralph Rice (no connection to the Ralph mentioned in the stories in this book) say there are two kinds of people in the world. One type of person can be described as a lark, and the other as an owl. Then he said, "God, in His wisdom, often marries the lark to the owl."

Larks love morning. They wake up cheerful and are very productive in the morning. The owl, on the other hand, wakes up groggy. He or she may even prefer not to be spoken to until he or she has had his or her coffee.

Forty-six percent of the people in the survey said that one of them was a lark, and the other was an owl. Seventeen percent said they are both early risers, and, a little surprising to me, 38% said both liked staying up late.

Here are some of their comments: "He works all midnights and has for many years."

"One is early to bed and late to rise, and the other is late to bed and late to rise." I guess they don't have a conflict in the mornings at least.

Another one said, "At first, I liked to sleep in on weekends, while hubby liked to get up early. That changed over the years, and we are both early risers now."

One of the ways to handle this is simply to respect each other's differences.

Rhonda is a lark, and I am an owl. After a certain time at night, I can wake up from some drowsiness and be quite productive up until 1:00 or 2:00.

When we were first married, we compromised and made bedtime at about 11:00 or 11:30. Now, Rhonda usually cannot make it through the 10:00 news. Sometimes I join her. At other times, we just kiss goodnight, and she goes on to bed. I would not describe myself as a lark, but I do find myself getting up at 6:00 a.m. if I have not already gotten up. I seem to require less sleep on most nights than I did in the past.

The most surprising survey result in this area, to me, was that one was described as a "neat freak," while the other could be considered as a "slob." Seventy-four percent described this difference.

That surprised me in that it was more common than I expected. It is kind of like "The Odd Couple" personified. I would like to hear more about how these couples handle this difference. The neat person will do well to cut the other some slack, but the "slob" really needs to try to improve, especially since he (or she) may not realize how pervasive this type of marital difference is.

Here are some other difference our couples discovered in their marriages:

"Rule-follower vs. Those rules aren't really meant for me."

"He likes the TV on all the time for background noise. I prefer quiet."

"He has always been much warmer than I, so he likes the bedroom cooler."

"One dried off before getting out of the shower, and the other stepped out on the rug dripping wet."

One who was in a second marriage reported a "difficulty in blending 'stuff' of households/finances.

One couple said, "We just got married after having children who are now teens and adults." It will be interesting to find what differences they may discover now that they are married.

One respondent said they had a difference when it came to "dealing with In-Laws."

Along that same line, another reported a surprise: "Married late in life. Wife's second marriage. What surprised me is the meddling mother-in-law myth is real."

While we saw some solutions already in this chapter, later in this book, we will see how some of these couples resolved their differences, or we will see some suggestions as to how those differences might be resolved.

We have seen some common differences in marriage, as well as some actual quotes from those who filled out our survey.

We saw differences in preference as to how we hang rolls of paper, squeeze toothpaste tubes, and whether we are early or late risers. We also saw how common it is for one to be very neat and the other one to be sort of messy. We saw differences when it comes to following rules, to having background noise or preferring a quiet environment, and preferences as to how warm the bedroom should be, as well as differences as to where one should dry off after a bath or shower. We saw difficulty in blending 'stuff' and finances, as well as a changed relationship with teens or grown children, and we saw differences of opinion as to how to deal with in-laws.

Next we turn to something simple to attempt, although it might require quite a bit of your time in some instances, but that will bring great appreciation from your partner. You might even have a lot of fun in the process too.

Your first action step is to write down some of your differences. Maybe you should have a discussion with your mate about this. Some new things might even come to light.

CHAPTER 3.

EXPLORE YOUR DIFFERENCES: YOU MIGHT FIND SOME NEW DELIGHTS

Would you like to spend hours together, enjoying activities you might not have known very much about?

It is possible for each member of a couple to allow the other to have some space for things the other person enjoys. That is fine, but there might be some danger of a couple drifting apart because of lack of time spent with each other.

Being open-minded and trying new things can sometimes bring some surprising delights in your life.

Ralph drove off in a huff.

"How dare she say that I don't care about her? Don't I work hard to put food on the table?"

He got ready to make the next turn. Then waves of guilt started overflowing in his mind.

Elizabeth had retreated to her garden. She jabbed the little shovel into the dirt extra hard.

"That man. How selfish can he be? Doesn't he know that I practically become a widow this time of year?

"Yes, isn't that what they call it? A football widow?"

She raised the shovel for another pointed jab. Then waves of guilt sailed over her too.

"He really is a good man, and I know he loves me. I just get so frustrated at this time of year, and it happens every year!"

Ralph turned around and drove home.

He got out of the car and looked toward the garden. His impulse was to rush toward her and apologize profusely, but his pride prevented him from doing so.

At the same time Elizabeth looked up. She wanted to run to him and throw her arms around his neck, and blurt out, "I'm sorry."

Instead she looked quite subdued—just like he did.

He walked toward the garden without speaking.

Elizabeth pulled off her gloves and rose to her feet. She walked toward Ralph, and placed her hand in his. They walked away from the garden. After several seconds, Ralph said, "I'm sorry. I realize I really do spend too much time watching football."

Elizabeth said, "When you do relinquish the remote to me, it seems like you get quite upset after about an hour or so."

"I know. You just watch those home makeover shows over and over. It seems like there is never an end to them."

"I don't want us to blow up again, but it is kind of like that with the football games. One gets over, and then there is just another one to start."

That day, they made a deal. "I will spend some time watching your shows, and I won't complain about them, no matter how I feel," said Ralph.

Elizabeth came back with her own offer.

"I will try to watch the games too. Maybe it would help if you tried to explain them to me without getting frustrated."

"Ok," he replied.

They really did keep their ends of the bargains. They set up a schedule each week. Elizabeth would try to watch a game with him every Monday night. He would spend an hour watching her shows too.

The surprising thing to Elizabeth was that she actually liked watching the games better when she understood what was going on. Ralph was patient too in teaching her. He had other games he could watch without interruption.

The thing that surprised Ralph was that they came across some do-it-yourself shows, and he really liked them.

He also allowed her to have more time for her shows while he just went and did something else.

It actually really helped their marriage. Elizabeth even found a favorite football team, and Ralph found a do-it-yourself program that he watched regularly.

According to our survey results, several people did try to learn about things that their spouses were interested in, but that were such things in which they had very little previous interests.

Some of the interests people tried to learn about had to do with watching sports. In fact, 63% of the respondents said they tried to learn something new about a particular sport or sports in general.

I do not know how many of the respondents were wives, but I suspect there was a greater percentage of those who responded to the survey that were the wives in the relationship.

Sixty-three percent said they tried to learn about a new sport. I do know of some wives who now have favorite football teams or basketball teams as a result of this effort.

In my own marriage, I have always known that I loved the sport of basketball. My wife did like basketball, but probably not to the extent that I did. One of my responsibilities while I was at Morthland College was to serve as the faculty athletic representative. I certified whether students were eligible to play. I also helped some students understand what they could do to become eligible.

I started attending the other sports on a greater basis, and have become more interested in them than I did in the past.

Because of this, my wife attended games with me when it was possible. While we both knew we liked high-school basketball, we did not realize how fast-paced (men's) college basketball was. We have both realized that it is about our favorite version of the sport—even above that of watching professional basketball. We attended about all of the home games, and we have driven several hours to go to away games. Rhonda would probably not have attended this much on her own, but we found these trips to be good ways to spend time together on the weekends.

Another person reported that his or her spouse was really interested in comic books and the movies that go along with them. This person could have said, "Oh, that's nice," and just engaged in other activities when the spouse spent time with these comic books and movies. Instead, though, this husband or wife (I suspect it was a wife) decided to try to learn about those particular characters and the stories that relate to them. This gives this couple an additional shared interest in their marriage, which is always good.

Then one person said that he or she tried to learn about playing golf in order to be able to share in that mate's interest. I don't know if they play together or watch the sport on TV, but I do know that it is commendable that one person would make an effort to share this with his or her husband or wife. If they actually play together, then they have a new activity they can share, that will be beneficial by providing exercise; and the activity may give them some joy as they see the skills of the "newbie" improve.

One wife reported, "I tried to understand his love for nature and my dislike of being outdoors. (I'm scared of reptiles.)" I don't know if this wife has come to like the outdoors better, but I am glad that she is trying to understand this. In some of these cases, couples will decide to let each have the freedom to "do their own thing." In other cases, they will attempt to do things together, even though one might have more interest than the other in those particular differing activities.

Another person said that he or she tried to learn about the spouse's love of fishing and hunting. I have heard of wives taking up the sport of deer hunting after they got married. Of course, this could just as easily go the other direction with the husband taking up the sport of deer hunting when the wife was an avid deer hunter.

Right after we first married, my wife and I spent some time on a houseboat that my parents had purchased. We had anchored in the lake and were casting toward the shore. There was a small tree growing out of the water. Rhonda had not been very interested in fishing before that. However, that day, she found that if she cast her line close to that little tree she would catch a fish. That was great, to begin with, to see the delight on her face when she reeled those fish in.

There was a problem though—not for her. It was my problem. You see, she did not bait the hook, so I was happy to do that for her. Furthermore, she did not want to touch the fish, so I had to take them off too. The problem was that she was catching them so fast, that I did not have time to bait my own hooks or do much fishing on my own.

So, I guess you could say that she discovered a new delight that day.

I occasionally fish now, but we don't really do that very much together. She never discovered the delight of baiting her own hook, or of taking her own fish off of the hook.

Still it is commendable that this spouse in the survey tried to learn more about fishing and hunting in order to share those experiences or to have intelligent conversation about those sports.

Then another individual said that he or she tried to learn about camping because of the mate's interest. While we laugh about the camping trip my family went on as described in the first chapter, Rhonda did agree to go camping a few times after that. I would say that we did have at least one successful camping trip, and I am quite sure that she agrees.

Another spouse reported that they, as a couple, tried to learn about new music genres. These had to do with music in church. One of the ways they are currently handling this difference is to go one Sunday to the first service in their church, and then on the next Sunday to go to the second service. Each of the services caters to each of their primary tastes in Music. I suspect that each of them find some songs that they like in those other genres with which they were less familiar, but they did not say about that one way or the other.

One partner has tried to learn about cars and airplanes. I know there could be some fascinating history about airplanes, and the story of flight in general. I have a friend who is in the process of building a small plane from a kit that he gained in negotiation to build a new website for that company.

Sometimes we have memories of favorite cars that we owned in the early days after we received our driver's licenses.

Others enjoy the sport of car racing.

Lots of times, in competition, it helps if you have a favorite in the contest. If you don't know anything about either of the participants, you can just pick one. If you and your spouse enjoy friendly competition, you might pick one who is not your mate's favorite. If competition gets out of hand for you, maybe you should root for your husband's (or wife's, if she was the original one interested in this sport) favorite driver.

This can be an additional way to spend time together, and, again, you may surprise yourself in having gained a new interest of your own.

One partner said he or she took up an interest in gardening after they married. This is certainly something that can present some tangible rewards when the harvest comes. In some cases, the husband will do the tilling and getting the ground ready, while the wife will do the rest of the planting and long-term care for the garden. In other cases, they will share equally in all aspects. The one who did not previously have much interest in gardening may enjoy some new delights.

While I can't prove that the majority of the survey respondents were women, I do suspect it was so. I was getting a little worried as I read the survey results. Then I came across a response that said the spouse tried learn about "watching home-makeover shows." The story about Ralph and Elizabeth at the beginning of this chapter illustrates how trying to gain an interest in sports and such shows as these could benefit a marriage.

Again, I can't prove it, but I highly suspect some respondents were husbands who said they tried to participate more in "watching romantic movies."

This is something I have tried to do in our marriage. No offense to Charlotte Bronte, I haven't really cultivated a great "like" for Jane Eyre, but I did find that I really liked a movie in which the main character was a young girl. That was Anne of Green Gables! I would never have discovered that delight if I had not tried to watch this movie with my wife.

In fact, while trying to spend time with my wife as she watched those romantic movies, I have also found that I like some of the Hallmark movies that also deal with mysteries. I probably would not have discovered those on my own.

Sometimes my wife will join me in watching science fiction, which I had a great deal of interest in during my teenaged- and college-aged years.

I was pleased to see, after all the results were in, about 25% said they tried to spend time watching romantic movies with their spouses.

Thirteen percent checked, "I haven't tried to learn about something my spouse is interested in." It could be that they are already interested in all of the same things, but I highly doubt it. Maybe some of these couples will try to discover some new interested just as a result of having answered this question.

Learning something new, whether it is a result of trying to find new things to do with your husband or wife, or for some other reason, always helps to keep your mind active.

I encourage all of us to continue to try to learn more about things in which our spouses are interested.

I have also learned that I really like going to garage sales or yard sales. We like to look for different things while we are there, but I have picked up some great "Self-help books" by going to some of these sales together. Sometimes, I will have a book with me so that I just go to the car and read it while my wife continues to look for more things. She has a wider range of things that she likes to look for. But I have discovered that I actually enjoy this activity. I don't think I would have discovered if I had not wanted to spend time with my wife.

We have found that many of our couples discovered new things that they actually like in the process of trying to learn more about the things in which their partners have a great interest.

Here is a challenge for an action step for each of you. Write down some of your greatest interests. Then switch lists with your husband or wife. Make a commitment to spend some time each week (an hour would not be too much) trying to learn more about that new interest. If your husband or wife needs to have some things explained about your interest, please be patient, at least during that specified time, as you explain the rules of the game, the steps involved, or the history of the characters in the stories or sports.

This could benefit your marriage, but it may delight you as you surprise yourself in finding something you like as you pursue these projects.

We have looked at our differences, and we have looked at the possibility of discovering new "likes" as we try to learn more about our differing interests. In the next chapter, we will look at differences that "make the world go around"!

CHAPTER 4.

APPRECIATE DIFFERENCES THAT MAKE THE WORLD GO AROUND: MALE AND FEMALE DELIGHTS

One of the most delightful things that God has created is the complementary nature of male and female characteristics.

We do need to understand that we are different. One is not better than the other—just different.

Each of the characteristics that come from our makeup as male or female has a great advantage, but if they are not understood, they may appear to our partners as disadvantages. In certain instances, each of those ideas is true. There are some things, because of how we are wired that are advantageous, but with those same characteristics, there are accompanying disadvantages.

Just understanding these differences goes a long way toward us appreciating each other more and more.

Such understanding helps us to keep from taking some things personally—especially when they are not meant to be against us personally at all. Such understanding also helps us to appreciate the good characteristics of our mates even more.

Ralph felt as though he were about to burst! He had been listening to Elizabeth for the last ten minutes.

What started out as a simple conversation with one statement was going on, and on, and on.

What was the point? Surely there was a point!

He thought back to a couple of years ago, when he would have half-heartedly listened to this barrage of words. He would become fidgety, and his mind would go to the remembrance of things he had to do. His impatience would have grown, and he might have rudely just walked off, hurting Elizabeth in the process.

Somehow, he learned that there was value in making the effort to truly listen during these times.

He might still want to tap his foot restlessly while going on this journey, but he resisted the urge for it to become so obvious. He also resisted the impulse of his mind to move on and think about the next thing that needed to be done. He brought his thoughts back into the listening.

So far, he had picked up five different ideas of what Elizabeth was talking about. His former way of handling this would have been to see problems related to each of those ideas, and then he would begin formulating answers to those problems. Today, however, he knew he was not expected to give all those answers.

Elizabeth began to realize that she was going on and on. She had learned that explaining the point of what she was talking about had value to Ralph. She came to the realization herself, and she stated a major idea of what she had been talking about.

"Ah, there it is," Ralph thought. "There is the point."

Elizabeth also had come to understand that Ralph always started out in "problem-solving mode." She did not always need him to solve the problem (but sometimes she did, and that was what she wanted in those instances.) She came to understand that Ralph did not intuitively know the difference, so she said, "Thank you for listening to me work through this. I don't really need the answers right now, but I do need to process these things."

In this chapter and some to follow, we will see differences that have explanations related to personality types, past experiences, birth order, spiritual gifts, passionate interests and so forth.

Some of our differences come about, however, simply because of the differences of being male and female.

Later chapters deal with differences in how men and women think—I mean the actual thought processes that go on within our brains.

For now, though, we will focus on some of the other gender differences that can bring us great delight if properly understood.

As we proceed, I must also hasten to say that in dealing with a topic of such complexity, that we must deal in many generalizations. Not all generalizations will hold true in every case, and, probably, especially in your case. Yet, enough of them will hold true, it will be a great benefit to consider them, as they will unravel some of the mysteries of marriage.

One of our differences comes about in the idea that we sometimes seem to be speaking different languages. In later chapters, we will be encouraged to discover our, and our spouse's, love languages. We will also see differences in the numbers of words we use to communicate, and the paths we take to communicate. This can sometimes make us think we are speaking different languages.

We also need to discover our different emotional needs. A later book in this series will deal with this topic, but we do need to understand our different felt needs.

When I do marriage seminars, I often take an informal poll. Each person is given a list of descriptions of needs, and he or she is asked to rank them in order of importance to them. After the lists are made, I ask some questions.

I often find that husbands will list admiration and respect higher than romantic needs, and that wives will generally list the romantic or feeling of love higher. Now, both need respect and both need love, but the ranking seems to come out differently.

Also, the men generally list the need for "sexual fulfillment" higher on the list than do their partners.

While these are generalizations, and there is nothing wrong with a couple that has these rankings reversed, the generalization is supported often enough that there is value in being aware of these differences. Of course, in your own case, you need to find what is really felt by your husband or wife.

It is probably true that you will discover different felt emotional needs.

The good news is that when God has a plan for a person to be married, there is value in the couple "becoming one." The different parties of the marriage complement each other, and if they are married, they need each other.

Dr. John Gray has pointed out some differences in his book, *Men Are From Mars, Women Are From Venus*. One of the things he points out is the husband is usually "Mr. Fix-It," while his wife forms a whole "Home-Improvement Committee."

That was why Ralph went into problem-solving mode when Elizabeth first started talking. He was being, "Mr. Fix-It"; however, as the conversation progressed, he realized he wasn't being asked to fix each item that was discussed.

Wives sometimes just need to be listened to, but they also would do well to consider to some of the suggested solutions their husbands might offer. Actually getting some of the problems solved will be just as valuable as being listened to when the problems are described.

Men, though, will do well not always to present solutions, but to focus on listening as their wives work through some scenarios.

The wife often becomes a "home-improvement committee" of one to help her husband improve.

While her husband may want to improve, he will likely try working through things himself first before asking for advice. Then, when he is ready, he will seek out advice from those whom he trusts.

Just as his offering solutions at the wrong time can have an adverse effect on his wife, her offering unsolicited advice can have a devastating effect on him. He has a need to accomplish goals and oftentimes to accomplish those goals without help. When he sorts out where he does need help, then he will ask.

The simple thing of asking directions when the couple is trying to get to a destination can come into play here. The husband may feel that it is important for him to accomplish that goal, and if the wife suggests too quickly that he might need to get some help, that can crush him. It is probably better to let him explore for a while and then come to the decision to ask for directions on his own. True, that might lose some time, but his feeling of value will not be crushed.

Sometimes advice over seemingly little things is very large in the mind of the husband. He may think, "If I can't be trusted to do this small task, how can I be trusted to do the larger things in marriage?"

Just as the wife sometimes just needs to be listened to, the husband sometimes just needs to be accepted and supported instead of being given unsolicited advice.

Understanding these tendencies can help us to cut our spouses some slack and help us not to take quick solutions or unsolicited advice personally, but understanding these tendencies can also help us to work on not presenting solutions or advice at the wrong times too.

A wife often has a particular challenge in a biblical marriage in that she is, at least part of the time, to be in a supporting role for her husband. While, this is true, she has a right to expect her husband to love and support her.

Another difference that John Gray points out is that "Men Go to Their Caves and Women Talk."

That just shows us that it is often important for a man to think through his problems before he speaks about them, A woman, on the other hand can process her problems while she is speaking about them, reminding herself of different aspects of the problem and exploring different avenues. It is important when her husband or friend listens as she goes through these different ideas in her mind.

The understanding for the wife is to realize that it is not a sign that her husband doesn't love her as he goes to the cave in his mind. While he is in the "cave," he is working on a major problem with 95% of his mind, and he may be listening to her with the other 5%. If she can understand that he is trying to work on two fronts that may help. She can be more accepting when she realizes that he is trying to deal with stress.

The understanding for the husband, again, is to learn to listen and focus his attention. He learns that when he does that, she often begins to feel better, and he did not even give a solution.

Dr. Gray has also said that men are like rubber bands, and that women are like waves.

The rubber band analogy simply means, at least in part, that a man feels a need to pull away and be by himself after experiencing times of intimacy. He needs to think for a while, but he will be back. When he comes back, he can pick up right where he left off. If they wife doesn't understand this need, though, she will not be able to pick right back up where they left off. When the husband understands this, he will let her know that he is ready to listen and that he just needed this time. This is a good time for the wife to talk. She should jump on the opportunity without having all the explanations of his temporary pulling away. After a good talk, then they can try to explore his need for pulling away. Dr. Gray describes this as: "A man automatically alternates between autonomy and needing intimacy."

The wife, on the other hand, is like a wave. She may emotionally hit a "high," and then start having feelings of self-doubt and come crashing down. When she hits bottom, she does some emotional house cleaning. Then, if she feels loved and supported, she will begin to rise again. When she is going down, it is difficult for her to show her usual love and compassion, but as the cycle progresses, she returns and is able to do so.

The man will do well by making it safe for her to experience these emotional waves. He cannot prevent these things from happening, but he can get better at supporting her as she goes through these times.

Rick Johnson, in his book, *Becoming Your Spouse's Better Half: Why Differences Make a Marriage Great*, gives several more contrasts between men and women. He describes these as "men's modes" and "women's moods.

One of these contrasts is in the idea of expressing love. He describes the man's mode as "Amorous: Never Give Up," and the woman's mood as "Romancing the Home." The man has a need to pursue the wife before they get married. He will do well to continue to pursue her after marriage. The wife's need of romance includes the home and the entire family.

Another of Mr. Johnson's presented contrasts is: "Work: Every Man's Bane, Every Man's Blessing," and the woman's "Nesting: Home Sweet Home." The man often finds his identity in his occupation, while the wife has a greater identification with the family—even if she works outside the home.

When it comes to play, the man is often in the mode of winning the game, while the wife may be more interested in just being playful. Some women are very competitive too. They will both do well to check themselves when they do not win the games. This is Rick's identification of a third contrast.

Fourthly, he speaks of: "Sustenance, Man does Not Live by Alone," and "Nurturing: Tending the Nest." Again, we see the greater identification of the wife with the home, and the man with things outside the home.

A man's mode is to be a "Protector: Guard at the Door," and the woman's mood is described as "Cycle: The Moon and Tide." While the man feels a great need to protect his family, the wife's need is to care for her family, and yet a cycle is in place. This can be similar to the "wave" Dr. Gray describes.

When it comes to a connection with God, the man is concerned that his life matters in the universe. He has a need for discovering his purpose—what he can do. The wife on the other hand seems to have a greater capacity for an intimate connection on an emotional level with God.

Finally, Mr. Johnson contrasts a need for friends outside the home for both the husband and wife. He describes it as: "Guy Time: Friends, Fathers, and Mentors," and "Girlfriends: The Sisterhood." While the shape of these connections is different, the need is similar.

We have looked at many of the differences that we have simply because of being men and women.

As I said at the beginning of the chapter, one characteristic is not better than the other—just different. Understanding our differences, however, will help us to help each other better as we navigate the waters of marriage.

A few good action steps to take as a result of reading this chapter are:

1. Men, learn to listen better without always going into the need to offer a solution.

2. Women, be careful about offering unsolicited advice.

3. Both men and women, recognize there are times for offering solutions and for giving advice—try to be more discerning about when those times are.

We have looked at some difference that were identified by our survey respondents, some surprising delights that came about when some tried to learn more about their spouse's interests, differences between men and women in general, and differences that "make the world go around." Next, we will look at not only living with our differences, but learning to celebrate them too.

CHAPTER 5.

CELEBRATE YOUR DIFFERENCES, BUT LEARN TO LIVE WITH THEM TOO: GO FROM ENGAGING IN COMBAT TO ENJOYING WATCHING FIREWORKS

You can't live with them, and you can't live without them!" That is a statement that *most* married people could make at sometime within the course of their marriage. The key is to keep that last part of the statement, "You can't live *without* them," alive.

Why do we find this wonderful paradox to be true? We all have strengths and weaknesses. We learn more about a certain person than anyone else on this earth knows. We see below the surface. When we do that, we uncover flaws. And, to make thing *worse,* that person also learns more about us than anyone else knows. They may have hard times of handling what they see. The frustrations of the discoveries of weaknesses may cause sparks to fly.

Many adjustments come with marriage. The "O" in the LOVING *way* to a successful marriage refers to "overcoming." We will look in the next few chapters at ways to overcome certain things we face. Although we are zeroing in on marriage, the principles that relate to

49

successful marriages also relate to any situation where relationships are involved: friendships, school, or work. All of us need to learn to overcome or cope with the differences of those around us.

Ralph and Elizabeth decided to attend a series of lessons in their church that dealt with marriage.

Ralph was a little reluctant to go at first, but he heard that some of his best friends were going, so he decided to check it out.

After the introduction, Ralph and Elizabeth both got very interested in the material, as it helped explain why they had the differences that were present in their marriages.

The first explanation had to do with differences of temperament.

Let's examine some of the various reasons for differences within marriage. Many of them do not have anything to do with particular motives that we might read into our spouses as being personally against how we are made up.

DIFFERENCES IN TEMPERAMENTS

Subconscious desires lie within all of us. The person who is naturally outgoing sometimes envies the person who can be more reserved. Likewise, the shy, reserved person often wishes he or she could be more outgoing. Opposites tend to attract because we see the strength of that opposite personality and realize that personality represents something we secretly wish we had within ourselves.

The well-organized creative individual sometimes wishes he or she could be more laid back. Sometimes he wishes he could do something "half-way" without it bothering him.

Therefore he or she is attracted to the person who has a more carefree personality.

We may think that a union of such personalities would provide perfect complements of each other, and they can, but it will take a lot of work for these unions to perform such complements.

Later into the marriage, the partners discover the weaknesses that accompany the strengths that attracted them during the dating period. At first, they focus upon the strengths of those personality types. As life goes on, they also become aware of the weaknesses. Each personality type that has its natural strength also has its accompanying weakness. The good news for the Spirit-filled Christian is that the fruit of the Spirit begins to work in his life. The Spirit-controlled temperament begins to modify the weaknesses. The Spirit produces within the Christian the characteristics of love, joy, peace, longsuffering, gentleness, goodness, faith, meekness, and temperance (Gal. 5:22).

The working of the Spirit, then, will not remove the strengths of the personality, but it will modify the weakness and will tend to draw the person to a more moderate position concerning his weaknesses. Therefore, the couple should understand the natural weaknesses each possesses and should focus on each being filled with the Spirit of God.

DIFFERENCES IN HOW WE THINK

Spaghetti describes women, and waffles describe men, according to one popular book that is on the market today. I suspect these descriptions refer to the way men and women think. Newsflash: Men and women are different! One is not better than the other—just different. Each has his or her strength. Together, such a couple can do a great work for God.

Spaghetti is pasta that becomes intertwined when cooked, indicating that a woman is able to think on several different fronts at the same time. She can cook supper, tend to the baby, and talk on the phone all at the same time without missing a thing. However, her thoughts may not always follow a sequential pattern. She can go from the beginning to the end, back near the beginning, then to the middle and not be confused. Such a thought process, however, may confuse her husband. The husband and wife must learn to communicate.

Waffles, describing men, does not refer to them constantly changing their mind—"waffling" on decisions. Rather a waffle describes the fact that a man can put his life into neat little compartments. For the woman, all of life may seem to be related, but for the man, he may see each part of life as being distinct from the other parts. He also thinks in sequences, going in line from one compartment to the other. Getting out of sequence seems inconsistent to him.

This compartmentalized thinking, however, can produce inconsistencies within him. He may experience success in one compartment, and be a total failure in the other. He may just block out the other. A man may not see an inconsistency by being unfaithful in one area of his life, but by being faithful in another area. Perhaps that's why sometimes people will sometimes say it does not matter what a public official does in his personal life--just. What he does in his official capacity. That relates to compartmentalized thinking.

Sounds made by young children have been the subject of study. The discovery was that young girls observed at play often used many words in making their verbal sounds. The young boys, however, spent less time forming words. The boys spent more time imitating the sounds that machinery or animals made.

Someone has indicated that we each have a certain number of words we need to get out in a day's time. The implication is also that a lady needs to get out more words than does a man. This, of course is a generalization, but it does match the study of the sounds made by boys and girls.

Therefore, it is important for the man to learn the skill of listening to his wife. He also may have to learn to organize the statements she makes into a sequence that will make sense to him. He needs to do this without belittling her. He will have a tendency to think that she wants him to solve the problem about which she is talking; when; really, sometimes all she needs is for him to listen to her. His job is to help her come to the end of her thoughts on that topic.

Steps to take to solve the problem naturally begin to form in the man's mind when he hears of the problem. He needs to be aware that she may not need those steps in every case. On the other hand, she needs to be aware that he may be able to give her an answer that will help with the situation she faces. She may feel better, having talked things out, but she would also do well to listen to his possible solution that he puts forth. His solution may be incomplete, partly because the information he gets from her may be incomplete, but sometimes it will be just what is needed. The wife who is listened to, and who listens to ideas given to her by her husband, will develop a greater feeling of security than will the wife who rarely communicates with her husband. The wise husband will soon learn that he does not always have to provide a solution, but the wise wife will take into account the steps toward solving a problem that her husband may give. If she discerns that he truly did understand the situation, then he may give her just what she needs to prevent future problems like the problem that gives her present frustration.

Demanding that your mate constantly work on his or her weaknesses can put a great strain on a marriage. The husband will begin to feel that the wife is constantly nagging him, and the wife may feel that he is becoming an unreasonable tyrant. One of the ways of avoiding doing this is to give our expectations to God. Then, when our partner shows steps of growth, we will not just take it for granted. Rather, we will be grateful for what takes place.

WHY GIVING OUR EXPECTATIONS TO GOD WILL HELP—
AND WHAT TO DO WHEN WE CANNOT

Giving your expectations to God will help. You may expect your husband to do something that he has not grown into yet. If you give that expectation to God, you will be happy for whatever step of growth becomes evident in his life. Likewise, husband, you may expect the wife to do certain things she has not grown into yet. If you give your expectation to God, when she does take a step of growth, then you will be grateful and delighted. You will not take it for granted because you will have given that expectation to God.

Since it will be nearly impossible to give all of our expectations to God, we will criticize and be criticized from time to time. We need a practical way of being able to respond to criticism. We will try to keep from criticizing, and our mates will too, but criticism will come. It is important to learn how to deal with such criticism. A few steps can help. When you are criticized, you might want to ask for details. Agree with the truth. Then you might want to speak the truth in love.

Asking for details will help you to understand if the criticism is fair. "What is it about this jacket that you do not like?" would be one way of asking for details if someone criticized your choice of jacket. Ask for enough details to understand clearly what the criticism is.

Then, agree with the truth. if your critic is right, you can agree and, if you intend to change, you might even want to state what plan you have for improvement in that area in the future. "You're right. I did turn hack in too quickly. I'll try to watch that the next time I pass a car.

What if your critic is completely off base'? You can agree with his or her right to an opinion, and then perhaps state your own opinion.

After clarifying by asking for details and then agreeing with your critic—where you can—then you might want to self-disclose. In other words state what you believe to be the truth or how you view the situation.

Away from the heat of the moment and perhaps the sight of an argument, it will help you if you try to look objectively at what causes your feelings of resentment, frustration or anger. It is easy to become defensive in times of criticism or disagreement. If things have been building for a while, you may not even be aware of what in particular is bothering you. Away from the situation, try to analyze what is frustrating you. Also, looking objectively at the issues will give you time to think through what you should say the next time you are faced with such a situation.

Overcoming differences will involve learning how to communicate with each other, and it will involve knowing yourself what troubles you. Then, after a while, you may be able to express to your husband or wife how something does bother you:

Another point in overcoming differences is to choose your battles carefully. You will need to learn to work on the major items first—while just learning to live and let live concerning minor issues. If you make everything a major issue, your spouse will be overwhelmed:

Peace will result when you learn to put away anger and malice. It will also result when you learn to forgive even as God has forgiven you. When you have shown much discontentment with your spouse and when you have created anger and malice and have failed to forgive, you need to confess the sin of grieving the Holy Spirit. Your peace of mind should not depend upon your mate's behavior. If you have inner hostility and anger, you need to confess this condition as sin. Then you will be in a position to try once again to restore peace to your marriage.

If you do not confess this as sin, you will continually think you are right and your partner is wrong. You will think all the blame is his. In actuality, you bear just as much responsibility to make things work as he or she does. When you confess your sin, you are on your way to removing at least one obstacle—your pride—to making things work.

Know that God wants to fill you with the Holy Spirit, and that he wants to give you the ability to walk in the Spirit. He wants to give you good things, and He wants to give you the ability to overcome the desire to fulfill the lust of the flesh.

Just as you know how to give good gifts to your children, God will give the gift of the Holy Spirit to you if you ask for Him to do so. Learning about the Word of God, and to change yourself based upon what it says, will help you to begin to walk in the Spirit. As both of you begin to walk in the Spirit, you will come closer together.

Both of you attempting to walk in the Spirit will cause each of you to have your own personal projects for self-improvement. As each one is trying to improve himself or herself, it will become less necessary for the mate to point out things that need to be changed. And, if you have given your expectations to God, you will be grateful for what is happening in your partner's life.

WORK ON YOURSELF FIRST

Conviction from the Holy Spirit is the greatest and most effective change-agent there is. Nagging often does little good and can bring about much resistance and resentment. However, when the Holy Spirit deals with the heart, then the responsive Christian begins to work on areas of his life. He does this from a point of commitment. This is why it is important for you to pray about your partner's actions. Ask God to show him his shortcomings, and when it happens, the person may decide to work on an area of his life. Then you can support him or her in the project. You may wish he had picked something else, but that just gives you something else to pray about.

The chastening of the Lord will also work in each of your lives. God's chastening is much more effective than any pressure you could put on your mate. Don't nag. Pray.

After you have worked on yourself and have looked objectively at what causes your feelings of frustration and resentment; further, after you have confessed your sin of grieving the Holy Spirit; then, after you have asked God to fill you with the Holy Spirit and have made a commitment to walk in the Spirit; and, finally, after you have spent much time in prayer, asking God to show your mate his or her shortcomings; then you might want to communicate with your partner about his or her fault. You will approach this time with humility. You will be working on projects to improve the marriage yourself. Then you will speak the truth in love—not with a haughty or belligerent spirit. Approach such a time with much prayer and have a commitment not to let it escalate into an all-out argument. If he or she hears you, agrees with you, and agrees to work on something in his or her life, you have the basis for improving your marriage.

Listing your partner's strengths and good points is a good idea, especially if you find feelings of resentment welling up within you. You might even want to write those good points down on a 3 X 5 card and read over the card several times during the day. When you get frustrated, you may want to read the card. We are to give thanks in everything. Sometimes we forget to give thanks in the midst of frustrating situations. Yet, we should do this because it is God's will for us to give thanks in everything.

That does not mean that we will be thankful for everything that happens, but it does mean that we should be able to find something to thank God for in the midst of our trials—even our marital trials and adjustments. Remembering your husband's or wife's good points will give you something for which you can be thankful. You will have something to be thankful for even when he or she infuriates you. Refusal to give thanks in everything is actually a direct rejection of a command of Scripture.

Making a commitment to start each day fresh will help. One way of doing this is to make a commitment each day to forget about past mistakes and sins. God does this for us. Why shouldn't we do it for each other? If one person in a marriage has created a drastic wrong, it may take a while for him or her to regain the trust of the other partner of the marriage. If your partner has wronged you, it, perhaps is O.K. to help him or her to be in situations where he or she can be held accountable; but the past mistakes should not be remembered in a way where they will be held against the partner.

Even when God says He forgets our sins, He does not lose His omniscience. He casts them as far as the east is from the west, as far as holding them against us is concerned. He surely, however, must know they happened. We, as God does, should cast our partner's past sins and mistakes into the deepest sea, and then we should put up a sign that says, "No Fishing!"

Realizing that every attractive personality type also has its accompanying weakness can help us to learn to cope with differences, Realizing that men and women have a tendency to think in different way may help us to learn to cope with such differences. The wise husband will learn to truly listen to his wife. The wise wife will learn to consider his suggestions for solving problems. Giving our expectations to God will help us to be grateful for the steps of growth we see in our mate's life. Working on ourselves first, before approaching our mate about his or her faults, will help us to be able to work out our differences. Being grateful for our partner's strengths can carry us through many frustrating times. Most of all, being forgiven and learning to forgive will help us to get along with that creature "we can't live with, and we can't live without!" Following these principles will help us as we face our partner's differences. We may not solve all the problems, but as the problems are still being solved, perhaps we can at least learn to cope.

As we learn to live with our differences, we change the explosions of combat to glorious fireworks display. We change our mountains to molehills. We learn not only to cope with our differences, but also to celebrate them. In the next chapter, we will learn to appreciate our mates even more, as we understand how they are shaped into the persons they are.

CHAPTER 6.

UNDERSTAND HOW YOUR SPOUSE'S SHAPE AFFECTS BOTH OF YOU

Criticism is one of the most frustrating things a person has to face. Too much of it can tear a person down. On the other hand, criticism can be a very valuable thing. When a person listens to his critics, he is in a position to see where he has been misunderstood if the criticism is not valid. He may also see that someone is just taking shots at him unnecessarily. He may, however, recognize that there are some good points in the criticism and take steps to improve.

In a marriage, however, criticism is often devastating to the spouse unless it is handled very carefully. It is more likely that your spouse will need a feeling of acceptance than a feeling of criticism.

When Ralph and Elizabeth listened to the material in their church group, each of them was reminded of times in their past when they criticized each other.

They had a discussion, and both apologized.

Then each of them decided to weigh their words very carefully before bringing up ideas *that might actually help their spouse improve.* They tried to speak respectfully and to find ways to bring up some of those ideas.

When you begin to focus on your spouse's strengths, you can encourage him to work toward greater accomplishments. Your spouse does have strengths, and sometimes those strengths are what drew you to him or her when you first met.

GENERAL CONSIDERATIONS OF SHAPE

Understanding his or her partner is the greatest challenge that anyone has in a marriage. Sometimes it is very easy to misunderstand from where someone is coming. Christians who are married will perhaps understand talk of spiritual gifts. Others, while not familiar with the term spiritual gift, will understand that we all have inner motivations.

For those of you involved in Christian marriages, if you understand how different spiritual gifts motivate people, you will come a long way in improving relationships with your spouse.

When you gain such understanding, your patience will improve. Sometimes all that is needed to improve a relationship is an improved understanding of how spiritual gifts affect people. For instance, a person who has the gift of mercy will react to a situation differently from someone who has the gift of prophecy.

If you were in a crowded gathering at a restaurant or at a fellowship at church, and someone dropped or knocked over a glass of water, those with differing spiritual gifts would react in different ways.

The prophet might say, "That's what happens when you are not careful." The teacher might say, "The reason it fell is that it was positioned in a dangerous way." The giver might say, "Here, let me buy you a new dessert." The server might say, "Oh, let me help clean that up." The ruler or administrator might say, "Susie, go get a paper towel. John, would you get the mop? I will refill the glass." Each one views the situation in a different way, but largely from the standpoint of his or her motivational gift.

Most people who have done extensive study on spiritual gifts say that there are at least two types of gifts: ministry gifts and motivational gifts. In regard to motivational gifts, they often say a person will have only one predominant motivational gift. The motivational gifts are referred to in I Corinthians 1:2-4. This word, translated gift, comes from the Greek word for Charisma Seven categories of motivational gifts are listed in Romans 12:6-8. The characteristics of these motivational gifts may not be evidenced fully in how well a person does something, but they do express themselves in what motivates a person.

The other type of gift is a ministry gift. These same Bible teachers often say there are many ministry gifts, while an individual has only one motivational gift that stands out. Ministry gifts are special characteristics that allow a person to accomplish a needed task. The S in SHAPE stands for spiritual gift. (We are using the acronym that Rick Warren uses in his book, The Purpose-Driven Life; however he does not claim to be original in coining the term.) Trying to understand your spouse's motivational gift will help you deal with your Christian marriage.

Helping your mate is one of your greatest goals. One of the best ways to do that is to discover the heart or passion that drives your mate's life. When you discover your mate's shape, you find what his or her spiritual gift is. You also look for the heart passion he or she has.

Once you find that heart, you have the opportunity to encourage your mate to grow. Sometimes he or she may be given an opportunity for something outside of his or her comfort zone. If it is not something for which he or she has a passion, you might encourage your mate to pass it by, but if it is something for which that person has a real heart, you might encourage her to go ahead because she will only get better by trying. In both cases their heart for the project should help them overcome their discomfort.

Just as the S in SHAPE stood for spiritual gifts, the H in SHAPE stands for heart motivations. When you understand these two areas, you will also know in what areas you will be able to give added support to your husband or wife. When they work in their "heart-area" they will often be fulfilled, but their motivation may lead them into uncharted waters at times. Then, you will need to give encouragement.

We need understanding in the areas of spiritual gifts and heart motivations; but, beyond that, we need to encourage our other halves to use their God-given abilities. These abilities may have been acquired through skill and much practice.

Purpose is the most motivating force in the world. When people have purpose, they can endure all kinds of hardships. The A in SHAPE stands for abilities. When you encourage your spouse to use his abilities in God-given ways, he will feel a sense of purpose. Those abilities may have been natural or acquired abilities, but the important thing to do with any ability is to use it for God.

We are always encouraged when we can be involved in things that we do well. If you look at your wife's abilities, and encourage her to use them, that will help her self-esteem. Likewise, wives, if you encourage your husband in those things he does well and show respect for his skill, he will have a feeling of fulfillment.

Sometimes men experience what is called a mid-life crisis. Ladies are not exempt from that either, but men often feel that time is running out, or they are concerned about whether they have made a difference up to this point in life.

Encouraging them to use their gifts and natural abilities to fulfill a God-given purpose will help them to overcome some lingering doubts that may develop into what is called a mid-life crisis.

The P in SHAPE stands for personality type. When you understand the characteristics of your spouse's personality, you are able to give space when needed. If you have differing personalities, sometimes you will know not to take things personally when your spouse acts from his or her personality type.

Knowing that some types of personality are better suited for certain tasks, you will be able to divide up the responsibilities that exist in the marriage. For instance, if one spouse is very good with details, and the other is not, perhaps that spouse should be the one to take care of balancing the checkbook for the family.

Knowing and encouraging each other's strengths will help you to have a spirit of cooperation rather than antagonism as you work through the various tasks that are required in marriage.

Knowing each other's bent will also allow you to participate in "give and take," and that knowledge will also allow you to "give each other some space."

Finally, the E in SHAPE stands for experience. We all have a history. We have had good experiences, and what we have learned from those good experiences can be used to help others. Along the way will face similar experiences in their own lives. That is easy to understand.

However, our painful experiences can also be used to help others. When someone is experiencing a particularly painful situation, someone who has been through a similar experience will be able to help them in a way that others cannot.

We do need to try to understand how a person's past experiences have shaped their personalities. Doing so will allow us to be patient in some areas that onlookers would not understand. On the other hand, just because a person has had a painful experience in the past, does not mean that they are not responsible for the decisions they make today. While we are sympathetic with our partner's past, we must also encourage them to live in the present and not allow their "victim mentality" to be an excuse for not behaving responsibility.

When we understand how our spouse's SHAPEs (Spiritual gifts, Heart, Abilities, Personality, and Experiences) affect both of us, we will go a long way toward improved communication and encouragement in our marriages.

Having looked at the SHAPE acronym in general, we shall also consider an additional factor that affects our personalities and motives. Then we will expand our discussion of personality types a little more.

HOW BIRTH-ORDER AFFECTS PERSONALITY

We just mentioned personality in the above description of SHAPE. We will now look more closely at some aspects of personality and at some things that develop our personalities.

Genetics, of course, plays a part in shaping our personalities, but some other factors come into play also. The environment always affects a person.

One interesting factor that seems to shape personality is birth order. People that are first-born children seem to share many characteristics. Likewise, those that are "middle-borns" share characteristics and, finally, "last-borns" also seem to share certain characteristics.

Of course, these are generalizations, but they hold true enough that they deserve serious consideration.

First-born children tend to be "super-parented." That is, the parents are extremely concerned about doing this parenting thing right. They read all they can (if they like to read) or listen to as much advice as they can. They devote a lot of time to this newborn. This fact of a first-born's environment often affects them in certain way.

Here are some of those things that generally hold true for first-born children. They can be full of energy and quite ambitious. Many first-borns can think quite logically, and they can become quite scholarly in their academic pursuits. They are often enterprising and have natural leadership ability. Because of all the attention that is thrust upon them by doting parents, they like to please people, and they may thrive on approval. In addition, they often tend to be (or feel like they have to be) perfectionists.

Diplomacy may be some of the greatest traits of your middle-born child (or children). Because of their position in the middle, they have a desire to see things go smoothly, and they also have to work at bringing themselves to the forefront. At least, they may feel that they have to do this.

All three birth-order positions seek attention. The difference lies in how that attention is naturally bestowed on each of these children. Since the first-born represents all kinds of new things in a person's life, he or she is likely to get a lot of attention in the lives of those new parents without a lot of effort. Since a last-born is always the baby of the family, and babies always seem to get a lot of attention, the children in the middle seem to feel the need to make themselves stand out.

This attention seeking can cause some things that almost seem to be contradictory when you are a middle-born child: You may be flexible, diplomatic, and a good peacemaker. Your desire for attention may show forth in contrast to your diplomacy if that desire drives you to be somewhat rebellious. Usually middle children have a tendency to be competitive even though they have a desire otherwise to promote peace and harmony.

Some Strengths of Last-Born Children become evident too. When you determine who the last-born child in the family is (by not having any more), you may see a "social butterfly" emerge. That child wants attention and gets it by virtue of simply being the baby, but the demands of the other children upon the parents can cause this attention-seeking child to learn ways to get attention when it is not coming easily.

Last-born children, like all children, are attention seeking. In seeking such attention, they often develop outgoing personalities. They also tend to be sociable and have a good sense of humor.

Many last-borns are idealistic, can be very sentimental, and at the same time very creative. My mother often likes to tell about the time that my wife told our youngest daughter to come in from swimming in our small lake to practice piano lessons. She came into my mother's house where our piano was located, and did not want to have to change clothes, so she got a plastic shopping bag and cut off the bottom corners. The she stepped into the bag and pulled it up over her swimsuit. She went to the piano and practiced her lesson. Then she got rid of her makeshift cover up and went back into the water. Now, wasn't that creative?

What about "only" children? They seem to be like a super version of first-borns. They magnify the characteristics of first-born children to a greater degree.

Some things that can cause exceptions to these general rules would be if children are born more than five years apart. In that case, the second child may exhibit the characteristics of a first-born. Another thing that can affect how a person may exhibit first-born characteristics, even though he or she is in the middle, has to do with gender. People will be affected by where they place overall in the whole set of siblings, but the first-born son, even though appearing in the middle (or last) of the whole set, may exhibit first-born characteristics and some middle-born characteristics. The same would be true of the first-born daughter even if she was not first-born overall in the complete set of siblings.

Blended families will tend to have children with mixed influences also. A first-born child may end up being in the middle of a blended family.

How does all of this affect marriage? If two first-borns marry, they may clash in some areas because of their natural tendencies to be leaders and so forth. If two last-borns marry each other, they may be doing a lot of negotiating and manipulating. They may be surprised that their spouse does not respond like people do in general to their otherwise influential tactics. Middle-borns seem to have some advantage because they are used to having to work with others

The key for help is to be aware that your spouse's birth-order has influenced how he or she acts and thinks. Then use that as a point of understanding your spouse. Rather than being upset, be thankful for their strengths. Then learn how to point out how certain things they do or say affects you. Tell them how that makes you feel, but do it in a non-accusatory way.

Birth order shows how certain characteristics generally creep into people's lives as a result of their home environments. Birth-order does have an effect upon personality.

HOW TEMPERAMENT AFFECTS PERSONALITY

While birth-order does affect personality, students of personality have also pointed out that people seem to have certain types of temperament, and these temperaments seem to be characteristics that they have from birth.

The temperaments have been given different names in the past. One set of designations was: Choleric, Sanguine, Phlegmatic, and Melancholy. Other sets of researchers, such as well-known Christian counselors, Gary Smalley and John Trent, have compared people to certain types of animals: lion, otter, golden retriever, and beaver.

Another way of describing the four basic personality types is to use the acronym DISC. "D' stands for dominant; "I" for influencing; "S" for steady, and "C" stands for compliant (or conscientious or careful).

We will use the designation DISC, but be aware they also describe the other concepts as follows:

D Dominant—Choleric—Lion
I Influencing—Sanguine—Otter
S Steady—Phlegmatic—Golden Retriever
C Compliant—Melancholy—Beaver

What are the characteristics of the dominant or choleric personality? How is that person somewhat like a lion? People with a D personality tend to be direct, decisive, and driving. They are good at pioneering new projects, and they place a high value on time. They may also thrive in going against the status quo. Some possible downsides to this personality are that the person may develop an argumentative attitude and tend to overstep their own legitimate authority. Their greatest fear is often that of being taken advantage of.

When a person's partner understands that this is his or her spouse's personality, he (or she) has a basis for giving some leeway when these natural characteristics show themselves. Likewise, when that partner recognizes his own personality as being dominant, he will also try to identify where he may be pushing too hard.

The characteristics of the influencing personality or the sanguine person show how a person can be like a playful otter. People with I personalities tend to be influential, inspiring, and impulsive. They can be very creative when needing to solve problems, and they can encourage others in a great way. They are masters at negotiation, and they can be good peacemakers. Some negative traits of these delightful personalities are that they may be more concerned with being popular than they are with correct results. They sometimes have trouble listening unless failing to listen is convenient to serve their purposes. They are not too good with detail, and they may overuse their gestures and facial expressions. Their greatest fear may be rejection

When you recognize that you have this type of personality, you can make a conscience effort to really listen to your spouse. When you recognize that your spouse has this type of personality, you can rejoice in the good points and watch for this spouse's potential weaknesses. Since people are often drawn to this type of personality, you will have to guard against jealousy of the attention your spouse gets.

The third personality type, the S, or the steady personality, which is called a phlegmatic personality in the temperate designation system, is compared to that of the dog breed, golden retriever. People with steady personalities tend to be steady, sympathetic and secure. They are very reliable and dependable. They have a desire to comply with authority, and they can be good at reconciling conflicts. They are patient. Their weaker points may show up in a resistance to change, being sensitive to criticism, having a difficulty in establishing priorities, and one of their greatest fears is that of a loss of security.

When you have this type of personality, you can be thankful for your spouse's strengths, and you can understand some of the things that drive your spouse. If your spouse has this type of personality, you can be thankful for his or her patience and ability to roll with the flow. Be considerate and help prepare your spouse for any future changes that might be looming in front of you.

The fourth personality type in the DISC theory is the careful personality. Some call this the compliant personality. In the temperate theory, it is often referred to as a melancholy personality. They can be compared to the industrious beaver in the animal kingdom. People with careful personalities tend to be conscientious, compliant to authority, and correct in their procedures. They are often very creative, and they can tend to be moody at times. They give a dose of reality to situations they evaluate, and they can be conscientious and even-tempered. Some of the downsides to the C personality are that the person may need to be given clear-cut boundaries and instructions. They can get caught up in procedures and methods. Their greatest fear is often that of criticism.

Again, if you have a personality other than the C personality, you may get a little frustrated if your spouse is taking a long time to do something because he or she wants to get things right. If you are aware of this as being your own personality, you can try to watch for the things that may be frustrating to your spouse.

If the two of you have the same personality type, you may see sparks fly when you both have a D personality. You may spend a lot of time trying to negotiate with each other if you both have I personalities. You may have a hard time deciding what you want to do when both of you have steady S personalities. Finally, you may have a conflict over the best way to do things if you both have C personalities.

UNDERSTAND AND BE GRATEFUL FOR YOUR SPOUSE'S SHAPE

Learn to value and overcome your differences. If your church has a class on spiritual gifts, you would do well to learn all you can about the motivational gifts of the Spirit. Be aware of your spouse's passion or heart for doing things, and be careful not to demean him or her for that type of motivation. Be thankful for each of your abilities, and use those abilities for the glory of God. Really try to understand each other's personalities. Just as you would do well to get information about spiritual gifts, you also would do well to make a study of personality types if you really want to understand your spouse.

Finally, be aware of how your past experiences (including birth order) affect both of you. Also, understand that your painful experiences, once you have come through them and overcome their negative effects on your life, can be used to help others. Once you have done this, you can see how your spouse's SHAPE affects both of you.

Understanding from where your spouse is coming, and realizing that one motivation is not better than the other—just different, will go a long way in helping you learn to live with that wonderful person God has placed in your life.

Action Steps:

1. Attempt to find your own SHAPE
2. Attempt to identify your spouse's SHAPE
3. Begin to recognize the positive aspects of the unique differences of each of your SHAPE

CHAPTER 7.

APPRECIATE YOUR DIFFERENCES IN EXPRESSION: DISCOVER YOUR LOVE LANGUAGES

Have you ever said something you wished you could take back? I think we all have had that experience at one time or another. That is where we end up having made unfortunate statements or a direct miscommunication.

This chapter will help with eliminating or at least understanding unintended miscommunication.

We have different ways of expressing our love for each other. If those ways are different, then we may really misunderstand our spouse when he or she attempts to communicate love to us.

Since we have a certain way of expressing our love, we probably also have expectations about having love shown to us in the same way. When our spouse does not show that type of expression, we may misinterpret that as a lack of love on his or her part.

Ralph and Elizabeth have two very different styles of communicating their love to each other.

Ralph likes to tell Elizabeth that he loves her. He thinks that once he has done that, he should be taken at his word.

Elizabeth has a different style. She likes to do things for people. That is her way of expressing her love.

Now, they both use words whenever they are talking about their love. Likewise, they both do things for each other as expressions of love.

Each of them primarily looks for an expression that is mainly like their own.

For instance, if they have a disagreement, after Ralph cools down, he will apologize, using his words.

However, after having a disagreement, Elizabeth may prepare a special meal for Ralph. That sometimes is her way of apologizing to him.

If Ralph doesn't understand that, he may not know why she doesn't say the words. Also, if Ralph does not show some type of action or service, his verbal apology may also be overlooked.

After several years of discussion, this couple has begun to understand each other's motivations. Ralph has come to understand that after they have had an argument, that Elizabeth is apologizing and expressing her love toward him by serving him in some way. He has also come to understand that, yes he should say that he loves her, but also she will have a great appreciation for him performing some type of active service in addition to his words.

Gary Chapman has identified five different ways of expressing love for others. They are: words of affirmation, quality time, receiving gifts, acts of service and physical touch.

LOVE LANGUAGE # 1—WORDS OF AFFIRMATION

Several years ago, in the first year of our marriage, Rhonda and I moved to Kansas City, MO. I attended Midwestern Baptist Seminary, and she had a job at The Baptist Bookstore in downtown, Kansas City.

Our agreement was that she would put me through school, and then she would not have to work. We have been able to keep that bargain. She does work now, but that is her choice, and she loves her job.

Well, she also did most of the cooking and dishwashing as we were establishing roles.

One day, I decided to stay home. I was not deathly sick, but I also did not feel like going anywhere. Two significant events happened that day. First of all, I got some much-needed rest and a distraction from going to school. Second, I happened to watch a rerun of a television program from my youth, *Leave it to Beaver!*

An even greater event also happened. My wife got home from work. I told her that I had stayed home.

Then she looked over at the sink full of dishes, and she realized that I was also waiting for her to cook supper. Then it dawned on me, that I should tell her how much I appreciated her.

I did tell her that (and my words were genuine).

She just looked at me and said, with much frustration in her voice, "*sometimes* I would rather have your *help* than your appreciation!" She was right, but those *words* really cut through me too.

It took us several years to understand the differences in our expression, and it was really helpful when she came across the book about the love languages. She tried to explain it to me. After a time of letting this soak in, and hearing about the concept on different occasions, we finally began to realize that was what we experienced on that infamous day of my insensitivity by overlooking actions that I could take to back up my words.

LOVE LANGUAGE # 2—QUALITY TIME

The second "love language" that Mr. Chapman identifies is that of spending quality time with your spouse.

This can be expressed by having times set aside to give full attention to each other. Providing special getaways, with perhaps an overnight trip, can be an example of expressing this love language.

LOVE LANGUAGE # 3—RECEIVING GIFTS

The third "love language" has to do with that of giving and receiving gifts.

The thought behind the gift is very important, and in some cases the expensiveness of the gift might be viewed as an expression of love.

Sometimes, others might misunderstand this idea as someone trying to "buy someone's love." However, for those who are motivated by this action, it is not crass. It is a genuine expression of love.

LOVE LANGUAGE # 4—ACTS OF SERVICE

There was another time in the first couple of years of marriage where we ran across the differences in our languages.

We had moved our first home, which was an eight-foot by thirty-foot trailer. It had just been set up on the little jacks that supported it.

That night it rained.

Then next morning, my wife woke me up with the exclamation, "Randy, there's water all over the floor in the living room!"

I am not sure what I thought. I knew that it was still raining. I couldn't fix the roof right then. I thought, "It is water. That is what we use to mop the floor. Even if we get the water up now, it will just keep coming in."

I may have felt that she was trying to boss me a little too.

She describes that as being the moment when her illusions about marriage ended. She said I rolled over and went back to sleep.

I'm sure I did later help work on the water, but her sense of urgency was probably related the language of "acts of service." I could have scored many points if I had at least done *something*, no matter how fruitless it may have seemed to me in the moment.

We now have a basement. We have had times of the basement being flooded. I have learned to take action as quickly as possible, no matter how overwhelming the task might seem. I think Rhonda appreciates it.

Those early marriage experiences illustrate our different love languages. Mine is words of affirmation, and hers is acts of service. Since we know this about each other, we can now meet each other's needs better. We also can understand how the other attempts to show love, and we can show our love in the language of the other one too.

LOVE LANGUAGE # 5—PHYSICAL TOUCH

The fifth love language identified by Gary Chapman is that of physical touch.

When my son was a teenager, we started a little ritual. I would bump his shoulder with mine. Someone had said that was a way that we as men could show our love for each other, and it would be equivalent to a hug. I thought he might be embarrassed by the hug in front of others. In reality, it turned out that we would do the shoulder bump *and* do the hug. The hugs did not embarrass him.

This past year, I had a conversation with him, and he expressed that his primary love language was touch. While this shoulder bump was something we did that would fall in that category, he also mentioned how he felt neglected in this area many times when he was a teenager. To my shame, I was not aware of it.

Don't get me wrong, though, our relationship is great, and he does know that I love him. He also has benefitted from our understanding of the different love languages—especially since I shared with him that mine was words of affirmation, and that when I affirm something, those are not empty words, and I really mean them.

KEEPING THE LOVE TANK FULL

Having recognized our different love languages, Bro. Chapman encourages us to "keep the love tank full." We can do this by learning our spouses' love languages and then speaking to them in those fashions.

We have identified five different love languages: words of affirmation, quality time, giving and receiving gifts, acts of service, and physical touch.

Here are some action steps you can take.

1. Have a discussion with your spouse, where you share with each other the love-language generality each of you identifies with most.

2. Look back over your marriage, and be grateful for where you can see where your mate attempted to express his or love to you in the language he or she identifies as being his or hers.

3. Recognize when your spouse is speaking to you in his or her primary language.

4. Knowing your spouse's love language, take conscious steps to express your love to her or him in your spouse's language in addition to your own.

Having looked at the various ways we try to express our love through the various love languages. Let's now look at something that can form very significant differences in marriage. That is the occasion of having a spiritual mismatch in marriage—either your own, or that of others you may know.

CHAPTER 8.

SURVIVE YOUR SPIRITUAL MISMATCHES

Corinth was a very wicked city. It was a very prosperous city in many ways because it was a center of trade. It was a very interesting city because of the diversity of population. When Christianity hit the city, it brought even more diversity into the lives of many families. Since Christianity made its way into a basically pagan city, mixed marriages developed when only one partner in the marriage accepted Christ. The church had much to overcome and much growing to do. As a result, the church was commended for many good things, and it had to be taught, instructed, and sometimes rebuked about other things. Part of their problems came about because of the spiritually mismatched marriages in their midst. If you have a spiritual mismatch in your marriage, then you need to do all you can to survive that mismatch.

Ralph and Elizabeth really did not have such a mismatch in their marriage, but one of his friends from work experienced that condition, and Ralph and Elizabeth were partly responsible for it.

Several times, both Ralph and Elizabeth had invited the couple to church. Ralph knew they did not have any church background.

One afternoon, though, Elizabeth met with the wife, and something in the discussion triggered an interest in coming to church.

Later she did come. The husband agreed to her going, as long as he got to stay home and rest.

She continued to go to church. Then she made a profession of faith and joined the church.

Her husband became quite fearful of the situation, as he did not understand what took place in her life. He felt like she was being pulled away from him.

Let's consider some of the biblical teaching on this subject.

Look at these words in **II Cor. 6:14-17.**

Be ye not unequally yoked together with unbelievers: for what fellowship hath righteousness with unrighteousness? And what communion hath light with darkness? And what concord hath Christ with Belial? Or what part hath he that believeth with an infidel? And what agreement hath the temple of God with idols? For ye are the temple of the living God; as God hath said, I will dwell in them, and walk in them; and I will be their God, and they shall be my people. Wherefore come out from among them, and be ye separate, saith the Lord, and touch not the unclean thing; and I will receive you,

Disobedience marks one of the ways a couple can get into a spiritual mismatch. This condition comes about when a believer ignores the command not to be unequally yoked with unbelievers. Though some would think that "missionary dating" might be a good idea, it is clearly warned against in Scripture. In this case, a believer ignores the warning, becomes attracted to a non-Christian, and finally marries the non-Christian. They begin their marriage with a spiritual mismatch.

1 Cor. 7:10-16

And unto the married I command, yet not I, but the Lord, Let not the wife depart from her husband: But and if she depart, let her remain unmarried, or be reconciled to her husband: and let not the husband put away his wife. But to the rest speak I, not the Lord: If any brother hath a wife that believeth not, and she be pleased to dwell with him, let him not put her away. And the woman which hath an husband that believeth not, and if he be pleased to dwell with her, let her not leave him. For the unbelieving husband is sanctified by the wife, and the unbelieving wife is sanctified by the husband: else were your children unclean; but now are they holy. But if the unbelieving depart, let him depart. A brother or a sister is not under bondage in such cases: but God bath called us to peace. For what knowest thou, 0 wife, whether thou shalt save thy husband? Or how knowest thou, 0 man, whether thou shalt save thy wife?

Another way such mismatch comes about is when the couple marries when neither of them is a Christian. Then, one becomes a Christian and the other does not. Again, this couple is in a spiritually mismatched situation. The one who gets saved is really not able to relate to his or her spouse in this area because the things of the Lord are spiritually discerned. The non-Christian just will not be able to understand until he or she enters into a life of faith, himself or herself.

1 Cor. 2:14

But the natural man receiveth not the things of the Spirit of God: for they are foolishness unto him: neither can he know them, because they are spiritually discerned.

Sharing exciting news with your mate is one of your greatest joys; however, this is not possible to do with someone who cannot fully understand how you feel. You will experience great excitement, but the other partner, to his credit, may try to share excitement with you, but he may wonder, "What's the big deal?" His failure to understand will likely dampen your enthusiasm.

This failure of understanding sets up areas of loneliness in the Christian's life. He or she would like to share the new and exciting things being experienced but will just not be able to do so. This will cause the Christian to have to spend time away from the non-Christian simply to be able to continue to grow in his or her life. On the other hand, the non-Christian may feel threatened and pull away from that which he or she does not understand.

The couple that once shared things together— perhaps even things prohibited by Scripture—will no longer be able to share a certain part of their lives. So, loneliness results.

New principles for living are discovered by the Christian. This will cause him or her to want to change his or her lifestyle. When this happens, further adjustments need to be made. These new changes will cause, sometimes, new areas of misunderstandings. One of the most prominent areas is the area of money.

The Christian will begin to read that Scripture says that those who give will be blessed in return. He will understand that all of what we have comes from God, and he will want to give a portion of that back to be used for the Lord's service.

The tithe, or ten percent, was the Old Testament standard. The New Testament standard is to give as the Lord has prospered you. Most Christians who really understand giving, however, make the tithe the minimum amount they will consider giving.

Wanting to give ten percent of the family income to the church may seem incredulous to the unbeliever. He may even say, as an excuse, "That's all the church wants from you, anyway—your money!"

Leaving is one of the fears that a Christian has. The fear is that the unbelieving mate will leave. Scripture even mentions the fact that sometimes this may happen. Then there are fears related to raising children. The believer, of course, will want the children to grow up to trust the Lord. He or she will be concerned that the children will rather choose to follow the unbeliever's lifestyle and belief patterns. Finally, and most important, is the fear that the husband or wife will never come to faith in Christ.

You see, even if the couple married in disobedience to God's command not to be unequally yoked, they still go through the process of becoming one, at least partially and in certain areas of their lives. It is almost unbearable to think of the one you care the most about not spending eternity with you in Heaven.

HOW THE MISMATCH AFFECTS THE NON-CHRISTIAN

Time spent reading the Word of God and attending church begins to draw the Christian away from the non-Christian. This can cause the non-Christian to begin to see Jesus as a rival in the marriage. To make matters worse, Jesus is a rival no man could match—although the non-Christian may not outwardly admit such. The Christian will begin to have at least part of his or needs met by Christ. The husband or wife formerly provided some of those things. Then, the non-Christian will see the respect that is given to the object of this newfound faith. A non-believing husband will be particularly vulnerable to a loss of a sense of respect. Some call it the male ego. Call it whatever you like. The Bible even commands the wife to respect her husband. That probably is because respect is one of the needs a man has.

Losing his mate, wondering what will happen to the children, and knowing he will not be able to measure up are all fears a non-Christian mate may develop.

He fears first of all losing his mate. There may really be nothing to this fear, but, on the other hand, if he views the things of the Lord as a rival to himself, he may have such a fear. This will often cause frustrations and crankiness that he himself may not be able to understand rationally. He just knows that he feels insecure.

Just as the Christian has concern for the children, the non-Christian will likewise have concerns. He will not want his kids to be "religious fanatics." He may want the moral training and character training the church provides, but he may not want the children to get into the things of church too deeply.

His other concern is fear of not measuring up. The problem is: if he is competing with Christ, he will not be able to measure up. He will not understand that Christ would desire for him to be all he could be, and that the Christian husband does not compete with Christ. Rather, a Christian husband tries to show Christ to all—and especially to his family—in his life.

Characteristics of Christ will begin to show forth in the life of a Christian. The fruit of the Spirit will begin to grow in that life. As the non-believer becomes aware of these characteristics, he begins to see the Christian as a mirror that will reflect the shortcomings of his or her own life. This will cause a sense of conviction—an uneasy deep feeling that something is wrong. That conviction is uncomfortable, and if the non-Christian does not deal with it by submitting to God, he will fight.

That is why sometimes a Christian can tell when the Lord is dealing with a non-Christian family member. He becomes miserable, cranky, and frustrated because he is not able to deal with the conviction he feels within his life. He may try to justify his actions. He may try to portray himself as a victim.

He may try to balance blame with blame. None of these things will work, so he continues to feel frustrated.

Similar types of things will happen in the marriage when one believer is growing in the Lord, and the other believer is in a backslidden condition. In any case, a faithful Christian may become a mirror for the unbeliever, and he often will not like what he sees.

HOW TO HELP YOURSELF IN THIS SPIRITUAL MISMATCH

Focusing upon Jesus instead of focusing upon your troubles will help you to live by godly principles in the midst of your spiritual mismatch. In other words, you cannot control your partner, but you can do all you can do to make your marriage—at least the part you can control—a godly marriage. By focusing upon Christ, you can bring peace into stressful situations. You can learn not to revile again when you are reviled. You can learn to show forgiveness. You can learn to do many things that would strengthen any marriage.

Discouragement will be one of your greatest foes. During those times, focus upon Christ instead of upon your troubles. You may have to consider your troubles to come up with solutions, but let the focus of your life be upon Christ. One of the promises in Scripture is to seek first the kingdom of God and then see how God provides for many of the basic needs of life.

Encouragement will be one of your great needs; therefore it is helpful to find the support of a good Christian friend. It will be best if this friend is a mature Christian, and it would be good if he or she had some experiences that are similar to yours. Most of all, that friend should be well versed in Scripture. If your friend does not know the Scripture well, he or she may give you good support but some very bad advice.

You need both: support and solid Scriptural teaching Sometimes even a small group will get to know each other well enough to share some needs. The person will share the needs, but he or she will be confident that those needs will be kept confidential. They will not be gossiped about, but they will be made matters of prayer.

You also will have a friend whom you can encourage. This will help you to feel useful while you are going through your own frustrating and confusing times.

Focusing upon Jesus and finding a good Christian friend can help you through your spiritual mismatch. Another thing you can do is to force yourself to remember your mate's good points.

Expectations are things that we bring into every marriage As a Christian learns what a marriage should be like, he or she will have to be careful not to let that new picture belittle his or her husband or wife. One of the things that person should do is to give those expectations to God. Then, when the mate does something good, instead of taking it for granted, he or she will be genuinely grateful for the good thing that has happened.

Aside from giving your expectations to God, you need to be aware of your partner's good points. One of the ways to do this is to set aside a time to reflect upon your marriage and make a list of your husband's or wife's good points. That person may at times drive you crazy. When that happens, it will be difficult for you to remember the good things you do have. If you make a list and put it on a 3x5 card or small piece of paper and carry it in your pocket or purse, you can pull it out and be reminded of the good qualities during your times of frustration.

How to Help Your Children in this Spiritual Mismatch

Values need to be given to your children. You will need to try to give them Christian values without turning them against your husband or wife. Fortunately, many husbands or wives will want their children to learn good character traits like honesty, hard work, submission to authority, and so forth. This is not always the case, but many times it is. Since the perception of Sunday school by many non-Christians is that you learn to be good in Sunday school, they do not have a problem with their children going there, just as long as it does not infringe upon them.

When a person has become a Christian out of a wicked lifestyle that was formerly shared by husband or wife, the task becomes more difficult. In any case, the Christian husband or wife will have to try to instill Christian values in the children without turning them against the other partner in the marriage.

How to Help Your Mate in this Spiritual Mismatch

Though you should first of all focus upon Christ, you also should make your spouse the most important human being in your life. Respect is one of the best ways of doing this. Respect your spouse's opinions and feelings. Try to understand what is going on. Time is another way of showing importance to your husband or wife, and showing deference to his or her wishes is another way of making that person important in your life.

In the area of opinions, you may not always be able to agree with your partner, but you can respect his or right to an opinion. You also can show that respect by genuinely listening. When communication skills are good, you also may be able to show another side to those issues without blowing things into an argument.

Deferring to the wishes of your husband or wife will make him or her feel important. You do not have to become a doormat, and you should not do all the deferring, but if you defer to your mate's wishes quite often, you will more than likely begin to find him or her deferring to your wishes from time to time too.

(When I am talking about deferring here, I am not talking about enabling your partner in destructive behavior.)

Another way of helping your partner in the midst of a spiritual mismatch is to give him or her forgiveness instead of what he or she deserves. God did this much for you, should you not do such for your husband or wife? God has shown mercy upon you. Do you show mercy to your mate?

True, you may have been saved out of a wicked lifestyle, one of which you no longer wish to be a part. You, then, need to be careful as to how you come across to your mate. He will resent your appearance of self-righteousness. He will resent what may appear to be pride upon your part. Yet, it will be very easy for you to see how far short of the mark he is. Instead of nagging, pray. Instead of judging, remember what God has done for you.

Forgiving time and again is important in any marriage. A young couple may hear the words "better, richer, and health" when the marriage vows are repeated, but they will likely encounter "worse, poorer, and sickness." Their commitment will be the only thing that will pull them through, and forgiveness is one of the things that will allow that commitment to work.

Learning to "fight fair" will benefit both you and your mate during your time of Spiritual mismatch. Do not withhold your physical expressions of love during your times of disagreement. Continuing to hold hands will help. Do something like this if at all possible. Learn not to exaggerate when you present your point of view and try to work toward solutions that will be acceptable to both of you if such an accommodation can be made.

Sometimes wives will use the physical expression of marriage as a tool to manipulate her husband. A husband may do this also. Fight fair without trying to use this as a major tool. Sure, each one must be honest about his or her feelings, and those feelings may cause coolness, but the technique of withholding should not be a major fighting tactic. (There may be times when withholding is necessary, but it will not because that can be a good fighting tactic.)

Also it is important to try to come up with solutions that will benefit both partners in a disagreement. This gives respect to both the husband and wife. If it is at all possible, work toward a solution that will help both of you.

Praying for your partner is always important, but it is especially important in the case of a spiritual mismatch. Or course, the main thing you would desire would be to see your husband's or wife's salvation. You will want to influence him or her most of all through your life, but there may come an occasion where you can share the good news of the Gospel with your mate. You will want the timing to be right, and you will want to be able to present the Gospel in a biblically correct manner.

Before talking to your mate, you want to bathe the situation in prayer. Then you want to consider talking with good timing. Timing can be extremely important. If your mate is quite frustrated or angry, that may not be the best time to approach the topic.

When the time seems right, you may want to explain to your mate that you want him or her to know the basis of salvation. You might want to take some of the pressure off of the moment by saying you just want to present the plan to him, and of course you know he is free to make his own decision.

Then you could read several verses of Scripture including the following set of verses, which has been called the Romans Road to salvation:

Romans 3:23 "For all have sinned, and come short of the glory of God"

Romans 5:8 "But God commendeth his love toward us, in that, while we were yet sinners, Christ died for us." ("Commendeth" means "commends, shows, or clearly proved.")

Roman 6:23 "For the wages of sin is death, but the gift of God is eternal life through Jesus Christ, out Lord"

Romans 10:9-13

That if thou shalt confess with thy mouth the Lord Jesus, and shalt believe in thine heart that God hath raised him from the dead, thou shalt be saved. For with the heart man believeth unto righteousness; and with the mouth confession is made unto salvation. For the scripture saith, Whosoever believeth on him shall not be ashamed. For there is no difference between the Jew and the Greek: for the same Lord over all is rich unto all that call upon him. For whosoever shall call upon the name of the Lord shall be saved." ("Thine" means "Your." "Saith" means "says.")

If your partner is ready, he (or she) may then want to pray, confessing his sin, and accepting Jesus as his Savior, his forgiver, and his Lord, or his leader.

If that happens, and your mate begins to grow spiritually, you will no longer *have* a spiritual mismatch!

It took some time, a couple of years actually, but that is what happened to Ralph's friend. He came to church for a while. He had several discussions with Ralph and accepted Christ.

Now, all four of them go to church together.

For further study upon this topic, I recommend *Surviving a Spiritual Mismatch in Marriage* by Lee and Leslie Strobel (published by Zondervan Publishing House, Grand Rapids, MI, copyright 2002 by Lee Strobel.)

CHAPTER 9.

IDENTIFY YOUR CONFLICTS

Many people have the mistaken idea that when they get married and enter into a state of marital bliss, that there will never be any conflict in their marriages. This mistaken notion happens sometimes, despite the fact that there is no other area of life where there is no conflict. For instance, when you are young and attend school, there are many potential conflicts that face you each day. Who has had a job where there was no conflict? Who has had a friend where there was never any type of conflict?

Maybe you think of the fairy-tale ending where "they lived happily ever after." Most of us know that life does not work like the fairy tales.

We are all unique individuals, and we are very grateful that this is true. Life would be very boring if we were all just alike.

Sometimes there is a common statement that is described as "the elephant in the room." That means there is something there that is obvious, but we avoid talking about it.

We have described our uniqueness and our differences, but we need to understand that some of those differences will cause conflict.

The first step to dealing with such conflicts is to acknowledge them. Once we get them in the open, then we can begin to deal with them.

Ralph was troubled. He realized he had backed himself into a corner. He had accepted several requests at work. Some of them required him to work overtime, and some of them were for weekends. Because of that, he was going to miss some of his children's school events.

Usually that did not happen, and he and Elizabeth were considered great supporters of these school events.

He wondered if Elizabeth were getting worried about this increased involvement at work. He could see potential conflicts, and he did not want the situation to escalate into a big argument.

Elizabeth had restrained herself. When she heard about the first few claims on his time, she was not worried. However, as she heard about the mounting tasks, she became concerned.

Both had put on good faces as they ignored the situation.

Finally, independently of each other, they came to the conclusion that they needed to discuss this.

He wanted to reassure her, and let her know that he realized what had happened and how this had crept up on him. She wanted to make sure that he knew about her concerns.

One night, when Ralph was not working overtime and when there was no outside activity going on, they found themselves sitting on the couch. The TV was on, but the volume was on mute. The children were in the other room.

"Honey," they both said, simultaneously.

Then they laughed. Elizabeth said, "You go first, please."

Then Ralph told her that he realized what was happening, and she shared that she had become concerned.

Each of them confessed that they put off bringing up the issue because of the potential conflict involved.

In order to deal with conflict, you first have to identify what the conflict is.

Years ago, I heard Charles Allen, the author of several books on prayer, describe his counseling ministry.

He said, "I have had great success in counseling people. They come to me for help, and I place my hands together, almost like I am praying. Then I ask, 'Now, what seems to be the problem?' After that they tell me what the problem is. Sometimes that's all they need—to clarify the problem."

He then went on to describe that usually, though, he needed to ask a second question. So, he would again place his hands together, like he would if he were praying. Then he would ask, "So, what do you think you should do about it?"

They would formulate an answer. (Unless they came up with something that was clearly contrary to Scripture, he then had a follow-up statement.) He would say, "I think you are right. Go do that!"

He had great success with this two-question method of counseling.

The first question simply got them to identify the problem or, in our case, the conflict.

In his book, *He Wins, She Wins: Learning the Art of Marital Negotiation*, Willard F. Harley, Jr. mentions several areas of conflict in marriage.

He mentions more, but I will bring up five of them here:

CAREER REQUIREMENTS AND TIME MANAGEMENT

This is the conflict that Ralph and Elizabeth identified earlier in the chapter. Sometimes this becomes a dilemma for one or both spouses because they realize the need for income, and they also realize the importance of spending time with each other and with their children.

When the couple realizes this is a conflict, they can then begin to take steps to deal with it.

Both of them might benefit from reading books or listening to tapes that have to do with time management.

They would also benefit by discussing priorities.

FRIENDS AND RELATIVES

When you marry, you come into a relationship that already has some established friendships.

Also, when you come into a marriage, you come into an established family. Now, your spouse can't help his or her family. In most cases, they have no choice in the matter whatsoever. (I say most cases, because they do have a choice to enter into relationships with people who have relatives by marriage.)

It is important to discuss how the other's friends have an effect on you. You are quite fortunate if all of your friends are also your wife's or husband's friends at the time of marriage.

However, there may be cases where true friends of your spouse rub you the wrong way.

It is very important to enter into a tolerable situation when being around those friends.

When you have a discussion with your husband or wife, you can take steps to limit the amount of time spent with friends that cause conflict for your partner. Of course, after you and your spouse's friend get to know each other better, the conflicts may disappear. If they don't, you need to recognize the area of conflict.

Financial Management

Conflict over finances is one of the most serious areas of disagreement a couple can have in marriage.

It is one of the most sited reasons for divorce among married couples.

Again, if there is this type of conflict, the first thing to do is to get it out into the open, so you can have a discussion about it.

Often, one of you will be a "free spirit" and the other will be a little (or a lot!) more frugal with money.

It will be very important to come to an agreement in this area. Some resources, such as *Financial Peace*, by Dave Ramsey, or *The Total Money Makeover*, by the same author can be very helpful.

Preparing a monthly budget will help. The "free spirit" often does not like to hear they word "budget," until it is explained to him or her that the budget gives them permission to spend money in certain areas. (That seems more freeing than emphasizing the aspect of the budget that limits spending in other areas.)

Children

Another major area of conflict might be in the area of raising children.

In my book, *21 Ways the Principle of Leaving Will Benefit Your Marriage*, I discuss several things about child-rearing.

One of the major principles, though, is that we are raising children to leave. They are to grow up, become their own persons, move out and accept their own responsibilities.

When that is successfully carried out, harmony between husband and wife can exist.

However, conflicts may not stop there. There may be conflicts over how much time is spent with the adult children.

Again, it is important to recognize whatever conflicts may exist in this area.

A quick tip on how to handle things when parents disagree on how to discipline the children is for the spouse, who sees the other spouse taking a stand, to back off and let the first spouse handle the situation. If there is disagreement on how the situations should be handled, they can discuss that later when the children are not present.

The important thing is just to explore whether you have conflicts in this area.

SEX

Sex is another area of potential conflict in marriage. If either party in the marriage had been sexually active with other partners that condition sets up possibilities of unfair comparisons, jealousy and resentment.

Even if the couple had only been active with each other, we are told that also causes some perhaps buried fear in that if they didn't respect the sacredness of marriage before marriage, they may question whether their spouses will be faithful after marriage.

There may be conflicts in the areas of frequency. One may desire sex more often than the other. There may be certain times of day or night that are not ideal.

If there are serious problems, perhaps counseling would be in order.

Some Christian books on this subject are: *The Act of Marriage,* by Tim and Beverly LaHaye; *Intended for Pleasure,* by Ed and Gaye Wheat; and *Sheet Music: Uncovering the Secrets of Sexual Intimacy,* by Kevin Leman.

YOUR CONFLICTS

We have discussed some possible conflicts mentioned by Willard F. Harley, Jr. You may have recognized some of those as being present in your marriage.

The most important conflicts, though, for you, are the ones that exist in your marriage.

I have often advised people in my talk about writing books, "You can't edit unless you have something to edit." Likewise, you can't resolve your conflicts unless you know what those conflicts are.

We have looked at several areas of conflict in marriage and encouraged you to acknowledge your own areas of conflict.

Here are some action steps you can take:

1. Discuss with each other whether any of the potential conflicts that were mentioned in this chapter apply to you.

2. Examine and identify the conflicts that are unique to your situation.

Once you have identified your conflicts, you can begin taking steps to resolve them

Sometimes such resolution comes about through the process of negotiation. That is the topic of the next chapter.

CHAPTER 10.

NEGOTIATE YOUR DIFFERENCES: TURN YOUR MOUNTAINS INTO MOLEHILLS

Having identified your conflicts, it is now time to resolve those conflicts.

One of the ways to accomplish this is through the art of negotiation.

Ralph and Elizabeth had a list of conflicts they identified through one of their discussions where they decided to talk about "the elephant in the room." They brought up topics they had avoided for a while, some of them for years.

They decided to follow some simple principles when they started their negotiations.

They would try not to interrupt each other as they each presented their cases.

They would not belittle the other one as he or she presented his or her feelings.

They would allow the other person to explore why he or she felt the way each one felt. They found that, especially in Ralph's case, he really did not know why he felt the way he did. He had avoided working through past issues. Elizabeth became patient and understanding, and really listened as he worked through the issues himself.

In less cases, but there were such cases, Elizabeth, likewise did not know why she felt as she did.

They decided to handle their differences in three different ways.

In one way, they would present their sides of issues and try to convince each other of the best course of action. Sometimes Elizabeth came around to Ralph's point of view. Sometimes he came around to hers. Sometimes they found they were at the point of gridlock.

Another way they decided to handle their conflicts was simply to grant each other freedom to be different and to pursue different interests. As they did this, they recognized there could be a danger of drifting apart, so they agreed to keep the lines of communication open. They learned to tolerate their differences in some areas. They learned to disagree agreeably, and they learned to cope with things that were not likely to change.

A third way of handling their differences was to compromise with each other. They learned the art of good compromise.

Chapter 11 will deal with tolerating each other's differences, and chapter 12 will deal with the art of good compromise.

In this chapter, we speak of the art of negotiation.

Sometimes one person will convince the other person, and they will get on the same page. Sometimes the other person will do the convincing. Again, they get on the same page.

Sometimes a couple will decide to trade actions. For instance, one may say, "OK, you have not convinced me completely in this area, but I am willing to go along with your preference here, especially if you will do this for me in (some other area).

One of the most important areas to be overcome in marital negotiations has to do with overcoming gridlock. When couples have learned how to do this on a large scale they have certainly made tremendous progress in their marriages. When gridlock cannot be broken, they will either decide to move on and cope with things as they are, learn to disagree agreeably, or they will decide to take turns deferring to the other in those areas.

Willard F. Harley, Jr. says, "Every conflict in your marriage is an opportunity to fall more deeply in love." Maybe that will give some encouragement for couples to enter into some of the harder conversations they dread starting.

In his book, *He Wins, She Wins: Learning the Art of Marital Negotiation,* Willard F. Harley, Jr. also states that "The win-win model for negotiation starts with a simple rule: Never do anything without an enthusiastic agreement between you and your spouse."

That rigid rule of consensus in everything may be too confining for some couples, but they would do well to at least come to this position in most areas, and to agree upon the areas where they will allow each other to do things without complete agreement on their parts. For this to work, they do need to be in agreement upon the areas where they will just allow each other freely to come to decisions without consulting each other.

In getting into the art of marital negotiation, the couple must first identify the problem. We discussed this in the last chapter.

When I speak of the couple identifying certain areas where they agree to disagree, I am not speaking of this as win-lose situations. Couples should really strive for the win-win situations that will come about when misunderstandings are cleared up, when they give each other a certain amount of freedom in decision-making, and especially when they learn the art of good compromise.

If everything in marriage ends up in a win-lose situation, where one spouse has to be a clear winner, and the other has to lose the argument, the marriage will be quite rocky, and the one who comes out on the losing side more often (especially if he or she loses a whole lot more than the other spouse) may reach a breaking point.

As you engage in marital negotiation, you need to keep romantic love in mind as you speak to each other. Sometimes you will be very passionate about the issues you discuss. It is important to speak respectfully and to not speak in damaging ways that will have lingering effects.

The win-win strategy is what you want to strive for in each issue, but sometimes you will do this by tolerating each other, not by changing your positions.

When you negotiate, really listen to each other. Think about how what you say will come across. Try not to interrupt each other. Try to see the other's point of view.

I mentioned earlier, that it might not always be possible to come to a consensus on every issue. You will do well to identify those areas where such does not have to be the goal. These are the exceptions to the rule in Dr. Harley's win-win model for negotiation (and he does indicate there are exceptions).

There are some common problems with conflict negotiation. It is very difficult to negotiate fairly when one of you is more emotional than usual. You should both be sensitive to the proper timing for your discussions.

Another common problem arises when neither partner wants to raise the issues. You need to face this as a real possibility and schedule a time where you both decide to bring up issues you have been avoiding.

Another common problem is trying to negotiate when one or both of you is indecisive. If you are the one in the marriage who is quite decisive, you really need to listen and draw out your spouse's feelings or preferences on certain issues. Your spouse may be quite content for you to decide most things, not having a preference either way. At times, though, he or she may have a strong opinion on the subject, but is not in the habit of speaking up. Be continually on the lookout for when that is the case.

If both of you are very indecisive, recognize this as a problem when it causes you to avoid certain issues. Come together. Say, "We are going to have to make some decisions (if there are things that really need decisions)." Maybe you will agree, "OK, you decide on these things." With each of you deciding in certain areas. If you do that, you need to abide the other's decisions when they are made.

Sometimes "doing nothing" is what one spouse wants. That sometimes may be the best course of action. If you are the other spouse, at least consider that "doing nothing" may be the proper thing to do. However, there are other times when "doing nothing" can be disastrous. If you see those pitfalls, it is very important to persuade your spouse by gently pointing out the consequences of this course of (non-) action.

Another common problem occurs when you try to negotiate when one or both of you is not enthusiastic about much. Again, just as when it is important to time your discussions when one spouse may be more emotional than usual, it is also important to be sensitive to your partner when he or she is less enthusiastic than usual.

We have discussed the importance of marital negotiation. We have talked about giving each other a fair hearing. We have talked about the importance of coming to agreement where possible. Sometimes in the discussions, one person will be persuaded to come over to the other's point of view. Sometimes, the couple will decide that there are certain areas where it is not necessary to come to a consensus. We also have seen that it is important to have a discussions at a time that is better for both couple, avoiding times when one is more emotional than usual or times when one is much less enthusiastic in general than usual.

Action steps:

1. Identify areas of conflict

2. Schedule times to deal with those conflicts.

3. Engage in discussions where you really listen to each other.

4. Be open to being persuaded by your spouse.

5. Identify areas where it is not necessary to come to a consensus.

Having moved on from negotiation: we will look at the value of learning to disagree agreeably or at least tolerably in marriages.

CHAPTER 11.

TOLERATE YOUR DIFFERENCES: LEARN TO DISAGREE AGREEABLY AND LEARN TO COPE WITH THE THINGS THAT DON'T CHANGE

Learning to live and let live is very important in certain areas of marriage when couples disagree.

Ralph and Elizabeth discovered a few of these areas. Sometimes in the past, those conflicts escalated, but as they discussed their preferences, they found that there were areas where they could live in peaceful coexistence.

Many who responded to the survey described areas where they had not come to agreement, but where they learned to cope with their differences.

When it comes to disagreeing disagreeably, one couple has done it so well that they came to a decision "to never argue." If you can pull that off, you will perhaps have an unusually great marriage.

We talked about some of the differences (in generalities) between men and women. One couple has learned to handle some of those differences by tolerating them.

They said they had chosen to disagree in "how we approach accomplishing things. I focus on one task and complete it before moving on to the next. She has ten tasks going at one time."

My son and daughter-in-law laugh about their differences when it comes to buttering toast.

Rusty likes to make sure the bread is completely covered from top to bottom, side to side, and corner to corner. Sometimes this can take a while. He likes it spread out evenly too.

Brenda, on the other hand, likes for the toast to be hot enough to melt the butter right away.

They joke about her jumping in front of Rusty so she can get the toast while it is still hot.

They have learned how to cope with this difference.

My friends Emilee and Curtis have a difference about being baseball fans. She is a St. Louis Cardinals fan, and he is a New York Yankees fan.

She posted a picture of their baby on Facebook in his Cardinals outfit. He posted, "No Cardinals fans" in my house.

Their bantering back and forth is good-natured.

You might as well have fun while you tolerate your differences.

Let's observe some more areas where our couples have chosen to disagree:

"I gave in to his, 'Those rules must not really mean me.' I understand now that there are people who view life like that that aren't 'hardened criminals'"!

Another area where a couple had differences that one spouse learned to cope with has a little sadness to it. "There was an activity I greatly enjoyed (practically lived for) before I met him that I found out after we were married that my spouse not only didn't want to do, but actively refused to even try. I had to give it up entirely. Still makes me sad 20 years later that he would not even try it once for my sake. He's nearly perfect in every other way, I remind myself. This one failure to even attempt a compromise is not a deal-breaker."

Here are some more:

"Organization. I am OCD. He definitely isn't."

"Money spent on kids."

"How to make rules for children."

"How we handled issues with the kids."

"When it comes to family."

"Probably how to raise kids (i.e. discipline), but not real big differences. Small things. Very agreeable on 'big things.'"

"Politics mainly and a couple of Scriptural interpretations."

"Level of involvement in politics."

"Politics."

"Whether cutting the grass is called 'mowing the yard' or 'mowing the lawn.'"

"Food choices: unhealthy vs. healthy."

"The debate over hunting animals. I try to get him to hunt with a camera father than a gun. He loves animals, but loves hunting. I think it is just a male thing. I don't get killing things and he loves the sport of it."

Another couple found a way to resolve one of their differences by making an additional purchase. Here is what one of them said, "Choice of movie viewing. Earbuds/2nd TV solve this problem nicely!"

Here are some more comments:

"The TV and music."

"He likes the toys picked up more often than I care about. So, I let him clean them when they are bothering him, rather than take that pressure upon myself."

We looked at the different ways the couples that responded to the survey reported how they learned to disagree agreeably. They found areas where things did not or were not likely to change, and they found ways to cope with their situations.

Here are some action steps for you.

1. Examine your differences.

2. Have there been frustrations for you that have not changed?

3. Are there things that are not likely to change?

4. Then try to figure out how you can cope. Can you at least tolerate his or her frustrating actions or habits?

5. Think about the examples of our couples that responded to the survey. Can you pick up some ideas from them?

CHAPTER 12.

PRACTICE THE ART OF GOOD COMPROMISE: TURN YOUR FIREFIGHTS TO GLORIOUS FIREWORKS DISPLAYS

Betrayal is often associated with compromise. Perhaps that is why compromise is usually put in a bad light. It seems to represent weakness. Perhaps a picture comes of a soldier who is tortured to give away secrets that are associated with vital interests for our country. Even if the torture is unbearable, there still is a sense of shame associated with "breaking." Compromise is also often associated with "selling out." Generally, the word carries a negative connotation.

However, in any home where peace and harmony exists, there is often a certain amount of compromise on the part of the two parties who are married. They may not even be aware of such taking place because they have learned each other so well over the previous years. Young couples that are adjusting to each other must learn the art of compromise. They must know when it is desirable and when it is necessary to stand their ground. If both parties are trying to stand their ground on every issue, sparks are bound to fly. Though compromise can be bad, it is also often good.

The way our government functions involves much compromise. The government gives examples of both good and bad compromise. Bad compromises take place when legislators throw moral issues out the window in order to pass a certain piece of legislation that will benefit their district financially.

But good compromise often happens. A bill will have to pass through both houses of congress before it becomes law. Sometimes the wording in the House and the Senate will be identical, but usually the wording is only similar. Even if it is identical when it starts, it can be amended in either house. After the House of Representatives passes a bill and after the Senate passes a similar bill, a committee will meet to resolve the differences.

This process often involves good compromise that refines the bill into its final form. If both bills are good, this works; however, if both bills are bad, then even a compromise of two bad bills can result in a final bill worse than the first.

Our government, therefore, gives examples of both good and bad compromise. Someone has said that our form of government is a very bad form of government. Then that saying goes on to say "only the others are so much worse!"

Ralph, Elizabeth, and their friends who were the relatively new church members, all realized the importance of working on their marriages.

One of the things that helped them time and time again was to engage in the art of good compromise.

BIBLE INSTANCES OF GOOD COMPROMISES OR ALTERNATIVE PLANS

We have several instances of "compromise" or perhaps better stated, "Acceptable alternative plans," presented in the Bible.

THE WILLINGNESS OF GOD TO SPARE THE CITY OF SODOM FOR TEN RIGHTEOUS PEOPLE COULD REPRESENT SOMEWHAT OF A COMPROMISE.

Acceptable alternatives sometimes are a part of God's plan. When the cry of Sodom and Gomorrah came before God, God decided to destroy the city of Sodom. Abraham began to plead with God. He asked him if fifty righteous people could be found within the city, would God still destroy it. God said, "No." Abraham continued to plead. Finally, he got down to ten righteous, and God told him he would not destroy the city for even ten righteous people. The problem was that not even ten could be found.

Would we say that God, Who is the same yesterday, today, and forever, was changing His mind? Was he compromising? Actually, God does not compromise. Perhaps he did not really change His mind either. Perhaps the full plan was "The city will be destroyed UNLESS someone asks for mercy." Since Abraham did ask for mercy, God was willing to let the alternate course take place. With God, it was not really compromise, but it did allow for alternate conclusions. In the case of human beings, arriving at such alternate conclusions would be called compromise.

GOD PROPOSED AN ALTERNATIVE PLAN FOR RECEIVING THE FIRST-BORN.

Another example of an acceptable alternative, as far as God was concerned in his command to the Hebrews that the first-born of every family would be given to the Lord, was that the Levites would be taken instead of all the first-born. Originally the plan seemed to be that all the firstborn would be the Lord's—set aside. However, God followed the same principle, but he allowed—actually commanded—Moses to take the Levites instead.

Since God knows the beginning and the end, this was not really a change on his part. It just represented the two alternatives that were always acceptable to Him but were revealed to man in God's time.

This was a more practical way of working out the same principle since the Levites would live in the same area. When human beings are involved in working out some practical things, change often does take place.

THE JERUSALEM COUNCIL, ON THE SURFACE, LOOKED LIKE SOMEWHAT OF A COMPROMISE.

Sometimes a compromise helps a party to discern God's will. A dilemma faced the early church when many gentiles began to believe in the Lord. The early disciples knew what to do with the Jews who became Christians, but questions came up when those who did not have Jewish backgrounds got involved in the equation. Would they have to become Jews in order to become Christians? These early Jewish Christians were enjoying their newfound liberty in Christ, but what part of the Jewish law would be required for the Gentiles.

Acts, chapter fifteen, describes the Jerusalem council where the early church leaders took up this matter. After some discussion, James proposed an answer: The gentiles who became Christians were commanded to do four things:

1. Abstain from things offered to idols.

2. Abstain from eating or drinking blood.

3. Abstain from eating things strangled.

4. Abstain from sexual immorality.

This was not just human reasoning in itself. God guided the process, but the process actually did involve discussion, reasoning, and coming to a consensus on the matter. The Holy Spirit confirmed that this consensus was right, and that the final result actually did represent God's desire for those Christians.

WAYS TO AVOID THE NEED TO COMPROMISE

While sometimes compromise can be good, there are also ways to avoid even having to go through the process of compromise.

IF ONE HAS NO PREFERENCE AND THE OTHER ONE DOES, YOU MIGHT AS WELL GO WITH THE PREFERENCE.

An easy solution can found when only one of the partners has a particular preference about something in a marriage situation. For instance, if one partner likes to sleep with the window open, and the other partner can sleep with the window open or closed equally well, they might as well sleep with the window open. In the areas where one does have a preference and the other does not, it would be good for the one with no preference to defer to the wishes of the other.

Deferring in these areas will eliminate the need for compromise. If one partner likes the paper towel roll to hang down from the front, and the other partner does not care whether it hangs from the front or the back, it would be good for the partner with no preference to learn to always hang it down the front. It will not be a compromise on his part because he has no preference. On the other hand, for the other partner to change would involve an unnecessary compromise of his or her ideas.

BE WILLING TO WORK ON TRADING BEHAVIORS.

Both spouses may have behaviors that are frustrating to the other spouse. Sometimes agreeing to trade behaviors can help them. An example would be for a couple who has grown apart in spending time together during the meals. Perhaps the wife has grown tired of fixing breakfast, and the husband for reasons of spite sometimes does not call her to say he will not be home in time for supper.

After discussion, and pinpointing the problem, they set up a chart. He will mark the chart when she fixes breakfast, and she will mark it when he comes home by 6:30 and is ready to have supper (or he will call in time to let her know he will be late.) As the week progresses, they mark off the chart. They then pick another set of behaviors and put those on a new chart. This process of trading behaviors is helpful to some people. It does involve the biblical principles of accountability and each treating the other person as he or she would desire to be treated himself or herself. This is not a compromise on a single issue, but it is an example of give and take.

DIVIDE UP THE DECISION-MAKING RESPONSIBILITIES.

A wise husband and wife will communicate with each other. One thing that can help to avoid compromising on many issues is to determine who will decide certain things. The couple divides up the decision making process. The advantage to this is that the process is simple. A family meeting does not have to be called for every decision. This process is quick, and it shows value to both parties in the marriage.

For instance, a husband may say to his wife, "You make the decision how you want the bedroom decorated. You decide the color of the walls, carpet, and so forth. (This is not a command for every marriage—it is just an example.) The wife then is free to decide without having to worry about what the husband will think. She probably, when there is time, will consult with him about several things, but the determination has already been made that she will decide. In this example, she may have said, "You decide on the outside of the house." He follows the same principle. (Again, this is not even a suggestion of how you should decide about your house, but it does show how one couple divided up the decision-making process.)

PRINCIPLES FOR WORKING OUT GOOD COMPROMISES

You may have implemented several policies that avoid the need for compromise, but there are times when you probably will have to go through the process. Here are some principles that will help in that regard.

BE WILLING TO DISCUSS MAJOR DECISIONS.

Wisdom results when a couple decides to talk over major decisions in their marriage. This will give the husband a chance to listen to the cautions of his wife, and again, it shows value to each party in the marriage.

Minor decisions may be determined by their prearranged agreement, but major decisions will involve the input of the other spouse. Even a major decision may have been predetermined that one or the other would actually make the final decision, but the process of consulting with each other is very important.

It will insure that all angles have been covered. If the couple agrees, then the decision can be made with confidence. Even if they disagree; at least the other partner did have his or her opinion considered.

If they do not consult, the feelings of worthlessness lack of value, and resentment can well up within the spouse that was not consulted. The husband does not want to come home and find that he (and his whole family) has been moved out of his house—even if that is the best decision to be made.

See if you can develop a "creative alternative" acceptable to both parties.

Resentment can be lessened when both parties start to try to find creative alternatives acceptable to both parties instead of drawing a line in the sand and taking a stand every time a disagreement comes up. Even the process of trying to find a creative alternative shows that each thinks the other's feelings are important. Also, certain types of preferences will be learned. When one type of alternative is worked out, a foundation is laid for similar types of future compromises.

The process also educates each to what types of situations will likely need to have such compromises worked out. Working on the present prepares for the future. Also, when your spouse sees that you tried to work something out for him in this instance, he will be more likely to try to work something out for you in the days to come.

A wife wanted her husband, who had no interest in church at the time, to attend special services at her church that were going to deal with the family on a particular weekend. He wanted to go away for the weekend. He was adamant about going away, but he saw that his wife really wanted to attend the seminar. Finally, they did go away for the weekend, but he also agreed to listen to cassette tapes dealing with the issues she wanted learn about. A creative alternative helped this spiritually mismatched couple. Within a few years, he did become a Christian.

TRY TO GIVE A WAY FOR THE OTHER PARTY TO "SAVE FACE."

When diplomats from opposing countries try to work out disagreements, they often try to find an alternative that allows the party that has to change the most to "save face." This shows a respect for the other party but still gets the desired result. It also takes into account the feelings of the other party, and it allows them the opportunity to work together in the future. Allowing the other party to save face gives you the opportunity to do unto others, as you would have them do unto you.

When a person is able to change his or her mind without being belittled or getting the feeling of "I told you so," he will be likely to be reasonable in the future, and if next time the other party is the one who will have to give in, perhaps the process will be done more gently out of gratitude for how the last disagreement was handled.

Even when a person has made a terrible decision, he should be able to get out of that decision knowing that his or her husband or wife will respect him or her in the days to come.

TRY TO EVEN OUT THE GIVE AND TAKE.

Always having to be the one to give in by one party indicates that something is wrong. There should be a process of give and take. Adjustments surely will have to be made, but it should not be one party who is doing all the adjusting. A wise couple will try to even out the give and take. "You give a little here. I will give a little there." This shows the personhood of each partner. If one constantly gives in, the other often becomes domineering. On the other hand, the one giving in may just withdraw from the marriage. Each should strive for a balance in the give and take process.

IF A MAN LIVES TO PLEASE HIS WIFE (WHICH IS A BIBLICAL PRINCIPLE), HE MAY BE WILLING TO CHANGE A DECISION BASED UPON AN APPEAL.

A wife is sometimes troubled when she reads Scripture passages that say she should submit to her husband or that the husband is the head of the wife. She can take comfort in the fact that she has a wonderful power, however. The Bible also says that the husband lives to please his wife. It doesn't list it as a command; it just states that that is how things are. Since a husband lives to please his wife, he may often be willing to listen to her appeals.

Also, a husband may have to appeal to his wife when she has been delegated a certain decision-making process. Or, he may have to appeal to her when she is rebelling against God's directives in their lives.

The proper steps to making an appeal involve coming up with a creative alternative. In the case of Daniel and his friends, the alternative was, "let us eat vegetables and drink water, and then see how we fare."

Then you need to give God time to change the authority's mind.

Thirdly, you should make sure you have the right attitude.

Fourth, you should be committed to follow through if the appeal is not granted.

What should you do if what you are appealing is something you cannot compromise?

WHEN NOT TO COMPROMISE

When should you not compromise? Moral issues are items upon which a person cannot compromise. That person also will not compromise when he or she is asked to violate a direct command of Scripture. He or she should take the steps of appeal just mentioned, but if the authority does not change his mind, then the person is free to explain why he cannot submit to that directive.

Sometimes a Christian will take a stand that will be misunderstood by those who do not know the situation. Sometimes a Christian's appeal will not be accepted. Sometimes he or she may be punished unjustly.

In those cases, take heart. Jesus said, "Blessed are those who are persecuted for my sake, for theirs is the kingdom of Heaven."

Be as reasonable as you can. Try to work things out, but, having done all, stand for Jesus. Just make sure that stand is right, and that you have a right attitude in the whole process.

God will not compromise when it comes to your getting into Heaven. Since God will not compromise on what it takes to get to Heaven, what should you do?

We talked earlier about some alternate plans that God had for dealing with His people. The whole of Scripture does show us, however, that God does not have an alternate plan of salvation. He will not compromise when it comes to your being able to enter into Heaven.

You ask, "Why would he not compromise?" One reason is that he is just. He will not allow sin to go unpunished. Another reason is that our loving Heavenly Father gave His only begotten Son that we might be saved. If there had been another way, He would not have done that.

Shortly before Jesus went to the cross, Jesus said, "Father, let this cup pass from me. Nevertheless, Thy will be done." If there had been another way, Jesus would not have gone to the cross.

There is only one way to be saved and that is to give your heart and life to Jesus Christ and accept His salvation.

You say, "But, How do I do that? What must I do?

You must believe on the Lord Jesus Christ, and you must believe it so strongly that this moment you turn to Him from your sins, and you believe it so strongly that you will spend your life, to the best of your ability, turning from sin to the Savior.

The Bible says that if you confess Jesus as Lord and believe in your heart, you will be saved. Have you ever really done that? Is He your Lord and Savior? If not, why not accept Him today?

When both husband and wife seek to draw closer to the Lord, they have more agreement in their lives. This, likely, will lead to less of a need, at least in some areas, for compromise.

CHAPTER 13.

RESOLVE OR MANAGE YOUR DIFFERENCES

We have come a long since we began our discussion of overcoming our differences in marriage. This chapter will discuss some more principles. You should read it for that, but, beyond that, I think you will be inspired as you read how many couples in response to the survey told how they resolved their differences. Over half of them had been married for longer than 15 years. Many of them have been married for longer than 30 years. Let's learn from their tips.

Ralph and Elizabeth were enjoying a date night. It is not something they get to do every week, but it is something they decided to implement as a result of one of their discussions.

They sometimes splurged, but they also just enjoyed spending time together at some very inexpensive fast-food restaurants. The time together was more important than the venue.

They appreciated what they learned from the experiences of the last few months, and they were glad they attended studies in marriage at their church.

Ralph admitted, "It was hard for me to sort through some of these things. Also, to talk about some of our frustrations was hard, and, as I discovered, I really didn't even know why I felt as I did. These last few months have been great."

Elizabeth agreed, "I am glad we made the effort. I understand you so much better now that we have realized the characteristics that generally go with our different personalities."

One of the survey respondents said, "He is very gregarious and extroverted, and I tend to be more introverted. If I'm uncomfortable with a certain situation, this helps me to better deal with more 'outgoing' activities that he enjoys, since I know if it gets to be too much, he will listen and compromise to help me."

Here are some principles that will help when you resolve your differences: turn toward each other instead of away from each other. Let your partner influence you, and solve your solvable problems

Here are some more examples from the couples who took the survey: "Learning to walk away when he was angry. Then come back to discuss the issues later."

"We had to learn that effective communication meant actually listening to one another and respecting the other's opinions, failings, etc., instead of seeing how loud we could yell at one another to get our [point of view] across. It took a very rough patch and marriage counseling to learn how to do this."

"Finances. A lot better communication.

Communication is the key in in any area of marriage, in my opinion."

"Taking care of finances; Took turns."

"Money management. She likes to spend a little more than I. We agreed any purchases over $100, we talk about it together."

"He doesn't like to be told what to do. Sometimes he copes and forgives. Sometimes I'm more careful with my requests."

"Stop getting cross at him for always telling me what to do, as I do realize I forget a lot now that I am older. By accepting criticism."

"I try not to correct his grammar and public. I will if he asks, but not unless he asks. We managed it because we respect each other's feelings."

"How to spend time doing things together instead of just being around each other. Examples: going for walks, going shopping instead of sitting home doing nothing."

"He spent way too much time away from home and family to go hunting and fishing. God changed that when my husband was saved, and he gave up hunting for attending church on Sundays. That gave us more time as a family."

"Spending time with children. I wanted to, and still struggle with my children coming first, and my spouse second, and my spouse often feels he should come first. I've had to become more aware of the time I spend with all of them and make sure I make time to spend with my spouse."

"We have soft music playing in the background most of the time. It satisfies his desire for noise and my wish for peace."

"No major issues to date. Try to deal with little issues before they become unmanageable hurdles.

Communication!!!"

"Living in Japan in a new culture and the way of living was a big thing we had to figure out. We also approached this differently as people and had to make adjustments for that. All the 'new' outside our house might've been a good thing in that it sent us back to each other. We became a safe place for each other."

"He is a talker, and I am straight to the point. I work on not interrupting him, and he tries to get his story out quicker."

"Different friends—we just give and take."

"Talk about how we are feeling, even if it is difficult to talk about. I finally realized he will never know if I never tell him."

"Arguing."

Action Steps:

     1.   Try to implement some of the tactics our experienced couples used.

     2.   Examine your marriage to see where you have overcome some differences.

     3.   Then discuss whether those techniques might work in other areas of your marriage.

     4.   Continue to have periodic discussions as to how you might cope, compromise, or do trade off in some areas where you have differences.

We have seen where many couples have made progress in handling their differences. Perhaps you and your spouse have made such progress also.

In the next chapter, we will see that it is important to keep discovering and working on your differences.

CHAPTER 14.

KEEP WORKING ON YOUR CHALLENGES: MAKE MORE MOLEHILLS FROM YOUR MOUNTAINS

Part of the reason that marriage is to be for life is because it will probably take more than a lifetime to learn all you can about the wonderful mate you married.

Likewise, since we are unique individuals, we certainly don't always think alike.

We should be grateful for where we have had successes, and we should keep working on our challenges.

That is what Ralph and Elizabeth decided to do in their marriage.

In the marriage survey, the participants were asked about their main challenges *now*.

Here are those results:

"We have our first baby on the way, so I expect us to encounter some situation soon that will highlight the differences that we have when it comes to child-rearing."

"The main challenges in our differences now come from how we were raised and what was expected of us. My husband's dad wasn't affectionate toward him and frightened him into behaving. My parents were very nurturing and believed in second chances and explaining why they wanted something done, or why something was wrong. I tend to have more patience [than he does] because he was raised to do something because "I said so.""

"Who's in charge?"

"Our Energy level is very different now. His is good, and mine is not, due to some health issues, which I am addressing after a long period of neglect. I worry that he will tire of being stuck with a sick wife."

"In-laws."

"Not a lot. Seems to get easier the longer you're at it. I would say [we have] some differences on what to spend money on."

"How much to save for retirement."

"We don't have any."

"None. Things have been better since we married."

"None. We pretty much always agree. We've been married for five years and have never had a fight."

"Money and how much freedom to give to our teenagers ranging from 13 to 19."

"Our adult children living with us. It does not bother me—not to say I don't get aggravated. However, he wants them out of the house. Also, he feels less of a man because of diabetes affecting his male organs. I tell him not to worry, that our love is beyond the physical, and I tried to reassure him"

"Adult children and how to love them. Schedules-- how to preserve our family with so many kids/School/ministry responsibilities."

"Worship styles: traditional versus contemporary. Workable solution for now is to alternate services on Sunday mornings. Sunday school and Wednesday nights studies are not an issue."

"Don't really have any differences now. We understand each other more and enjoy spending time together doing the things we have in common."

"None. We both act like Christens and try to put the other person first as well as trying to see things from their point of view."

"Trusting the Lord and my husband to lead and look after our family."

"Is our mission field now here in our local church/community, or back in Africa?"

"Letting stress affect our lives."

CONCLUSION

In any marriage, it is important to identify conflicts. It is important to learn to really listen to each other. It is important to understand the many factors that make us different.

Once we identify the conflicts, we have some choices of action:

1. We can live and let live. We can simply let our partners be who they really are, while they afford us the same privilege.

2. We can negotiate our differences and the actions we should take because of them.

3. We can engage in the art of good compromise.

4. We can decide to "trade off" in certain areas.

5. We can decide to tolerate and cope with the things that are not likely to change.

6. We can celebrate our differences.

When we do this, our mountains will truly be changed to molehills.

The first book in this series dealt with "Leaving," which represents the most important "Move" you can make in your marriage.

This book dealt with "Overcoming," which represents the most important "Commitment" you can make in your marriage.

The next book will deal with "Valuing," which forms the most important "Attitude" you can cultivate in your marriage. When both of you develop this attitude, you both will feel really special, and you will be highly encouraged as you move on to a state of marital bliss.

ABOUT THE AUTHOR

Dr. Randy Carney is the Amazon best-selling author of *21 Ways the Principle of Leaving Will Benefit Your Marriage*. He is also the author of the now out-of-print: *The LOVING Way to a Successful Marriage: Six Keys to Marital Bliss.* That original book forms the basis for this present series of Books: The LOVING Way Series. The current book is the second in the series. He lives in Thompsonville, IL, with his wife, Rhonda. Randy loves educating and inspiring other authors, speakers and entrepreneurs to succeed and live the life of their dreams.

Randy often speaks on the topics of marriage, writing, and leadership. His signature talk is: "How to Write a Book in 28 Days or Less, Without Stressing Yourself to Death." As a book-writing coach, he specializes in helping speakers and aspiring authors get their books written and published.

Learn more about Randy as an author at amazon.com/author/randycarney

Learn more about Randy's writing, coaching and speaking enterprises at www.RandyCarneySpeaker.com.

OTHER BOOKS BY DR. RANDY CARNEY

The LOVING Way to a Successful Marriage: Six Keys to Marital Bliss. This book is currently out of print. Limited quantities are available. If you would like more information email me at rcarney6@gmail.com.

21 Ways the Principle of Leaving Will Benefit Your Marriage: Why You Should Apply this Shocking Principle to Your Marriage. This is available in a Kindle edition. This is also volume 1 in The LOVING Way Series.

21 Ways the Principle of Leaving Will Benefit Your Marriage: Why You Should Apply this Shocking Principle to Your Marriage. This is also the title of the Paperback version.

What Others Are Saying About Randy's Books and Speaking

ABC's Secret Millionaire James Malinchak, Supports Randy's Message **Noted TV Personality and Professional Speaker James Malinchak**

"The information on personality and how men and women think in *The LOVING Way to a Successful Marriage: Six Keys to Marital Bliss* is worth the investment in this book many times over.

–James Malinchak
Featured on ABC's Hit TV Show, "Secret Millionaire"
Founder, www.BigMoneySpeaker.com

Elementary and High-School Students

"Dr. Carney, I loved it when you talked about camping and dating. That was hilarious!" –Hanna

"Two Dates or Less--I enjoyed it and plan on using it in the future. P.S. I plan on using the water trick in the tent if I need to."--J. B.

Adults

"Even though I'm single, I appreciated the message. It gave me info on things/attributes to look for and expect should the Lord send me a Christian spouse in the future."–Lisa Jones

"This was a good program! I loved the scale for the 10 items important in a marriage. I am excited to meet the needs with my husband. Thanks for showing us a great relationship! "–Renee Anderson

151

"Men's Breakout was excellent. Questions and discussion in Breakout sessions could be interesting."–Mike Meece

A University President

Dr. James Flanagan, President, Luther Rice Seminary and University

"Dr. Randy Carney and I have had the privilege to grow up in the same community, attend the same church, and to be called into the gospel ministry. Randy has spiritual discernment and a gift of encouragement. Dr. Carney's suggestions for balance across six critical areas of relationships will benefit any marriage. When applied by both husband and wife, they can very well indeed be 'six keys for marital bliss!'"

–Dr. James Flanagan, President
Luther Rice Seminary and University

A Pastor

"To help [the couples and families of my congregation], I have called on Dr. Carney to facilitate a marriage enrichment seminar at our church. I could not have been more pleased or blessed by how he and his wife ministered to and encouraged our church family."

–John Robinson, Pastor,
First Baptist Church of Thompsonville, IL.

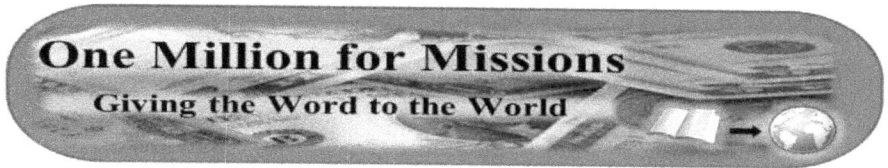

Randy Carney, President
Rhonda Carney, Vice-President

21086 Number 9 Blacktop
Thompsonville, IL 62890
www.RandyCarneySpeaker.com
E-Mail Address: rcarney6@gmail.com
Phone: 618-218-4271

The One Million for Missions Project

This is a non-profit organization founded by Randy and Rhonda Carney as part of Rhonda's response to impressions received during one of her regular prayer times.

You Can Help by Being a Co-Author

Rhonda was impressed to gather people's stories in order to write a book on ***God's Surprises.*** Please send us your stories to the above addresses. We will edit them lightly, publish them on the website, http://OneMillionforMissions.com, and choose some to include in the book. If yours is chosen, you will retain the copyright, and you will also grant One Million for Missions permission to publish the story in various forms in the book and any spinoff projects.

We prefer stories about two to three pages in length, but we will publish some that might be longer if they fit well with the project. The stories should be encouraging and tell about unusual ways God has "come through for you" in your life. Many times these provisions come at the last minute when it comes to God's timing.

All proceeds above expenses from income from those books will go to missions.

Also, that which comes in for marriage seminars and speaking engagements will go toward this project.

Who will benefit? All of the following will benefit: Your denominational mission board, independent missions supported by your church, Rusty and Brenda Carney of Free Will Baptist International Missions, Children's International Lifeline, and Many Hands of Christ as well as mission projects initiated by One Million for Missions.

Another Way You Can Help

Sponsor a marriage seminar, and we will donate half (above expenses) to your mission project, with the rest going to One Million for Missions. Ten percent of any proceeds that come from people investing in continuing education materials at the back of the room will also go to your mission project.

To Contact Dr. Carney for Speaking Engagements,

Please read the information at
http://www.RandyCarneySpeaker.com and contact him as
listed on the previous page.

Notice the special provisions made for churches and non-profit organizations.

You can also read about Randy's speaking projects at
http://www.SpeakerMatch.com and
http://www.freespeakerbureau.com.

ONE LAST THING...

If you enjoyed this book or found it useful I'd be very grateful if you'd post a short review on Amazon. Your support really does make a difference, and I read all the reviews personally so I can get your feedback and make this and future books even better.

If you'd like to leave a review then all you need to do is click the review link on this book's page on Amazon.

Thanks again for your support!

www.ingramcontent.com/pod-product-compliance
Lightning Source LLC
Chambersburg PA
CBHW060930040426
42445CB00011B/879